AQA Religious Studies B

Religious Philosophy and Ultimate Questions

GCSE

Marianne Fleming

Anne Jordan

Peter Smith

David Worden

Series editor

Cynthia Bartlett

Nelson Thornes

Published in 2009 by:
Nelson Thornes Ltd
Delta Place
27 Bath Road
CHELTENHAM
GL53 7TH
United Kingdom

09 10 11 12 13 / 10 9 8 7 6 5 4 3 2 1

A catalogue record for this book is available from the British Library

ISBN 978 1 4085 0515 1

Cover photograph/illustration by Alamy/ Digital Vision ANK9PJ
Illustrations by Paul McCaffrey
Page make-up by Pantek

Printed and bound in Spain by GraphyCems

Photo acknowledgements

Alamy: ArkReligion.com / 5.1C; Mary Evans Picture Library / 1.9A; Neil McAllister / 5.5B; The London Art Archive / 1.2B; 1.4A; 3.4B; Tim Gainey / 3.2B; World Religions Photo Library / 5.5C; **AP Photos:** Andy Wong / 5.9B; Shizou Kambayashi / 5.4B; **Corbis:** Bettmann / 3.10B; Christie's Images / 5.10A; Dai Kurokawa / epa / 2.2B; Franz-Peter Tschauner / dpa / 1.7A; Images.com / 4.6B; Tom Brakefield / 1.10A; **Ellen G. White Estate, Inc.:** 2.9A; **Fotolia:** 1.2A; 1.6A; 1.6B; 1.10A; 2.3A; 2.4B; 2.4C; 2.6A; 2.7A; 3.2A; 3.4A; 3.7A; 3.8B; 3.9A; 3.9B; 3.11A; 4.1A; 4.1B; 4.3A; 4.7A; 4.8A; 4.9A; 5.1A; 5.1B; 5.2A; 5.3A; 5.4A; 5.4C; 5.6B; 5.7A; 5.7B; 5.8B; 5.9A; 6.2A; 6.3C; 6.4B; 6.5A; 6.7A; 6.7B; 6.7C; **Getty Images:** AFP / 1.5A; Keystone / 3.6A; 3.10A; Stock Montage / 1.1A; **iStockphoto:** 1.1B; 2.1A; 2.1B; 2.2A; 2.3B; 2.4A; 2.7B; 2.7C; 2.8A; 2.10A; 2.10B; 2.10C; 2.10D; 2.10E; 2.10F; 2.11A; 3.3A; 3.3B; 3.3C; 3.8A; 4.1C; 4.3B; 4.5B; 4.7B; 4.8B; 4.9B; 4.10A; 5.2B; 5.5A; 5.6A; 5.6C; 5.8A; 5.8C; 5.10C; 6.1A; 6.1B; 6.3A; 6.3B; 6.5B; 6.6A; 6.6B; 6.6C; 6.9A; 6.9B; 6.9C; 6.10A; 6.10B; 6.11A; **Mary Evans Picture Library:** 6.8B; **Muslim Aid:** 3.5A; **NASA:** Paul Alers / 6.2B; **Newberry Library:** SuperStock / 4.2A; **Reuters:** Luis Enrique Ascui / SM / 3.1A; **Science Photo Library:** Manfred Kage / 4.4A; **The Bridgeman Art Library:** 4.10B; 6.4A; Ann & Burg Peerless Picture Library / Private Collection / 1.2C; 1.3A

Text acknowledgements

2.1, 2.5, 4.5, 4.10, 5.5, 6.3: Extracts from *THE HOLY QURAN TRANSLATION AND COMMENTARY* by Abdullah Yusuf Ali, Reprinted with permission of IPCI - Islamic Vision, 434 Coventry Road, Small Heath, Birmingham B10 0UG UK 2.9: 'The Revelation of Ellen White', The Times, 17 April 2003. 3.1: 'China earthquake kills thousands' by Elizabeth Stewart, The Guardian, 12 May 2008. Reprinted with permission. 3.6: 'Angelika Kluk murder: Judge sentences student's killer to life for "inhuman" and "evil" attack' by Esther Addley, The Guardian, 05 May 2007. Reprinted with permission. 'Groom tried to fight off attackers in Antigua killing' by Anil Dawar, The Guardian, 30 July 2008. Reprinted with permission. 'China accuses US of trying to sabotage Olympics' by Jonathan Watts, The Guardian, 31 July 2008. Reprinted with permission. 'Beyond good and evil' by Rowenna Davis, The Guardian, 12 May 2008. Reprinted with permission. 4.8: River out of Eden by Richard Dawkins Harper Collins 1995. 5.9: Dalai Lama quotation on the guru from http://encyclopedia.stateuniversity.com/pages/9247/guru.html 6.8: Richard Dawkins quote from his website http://www.simonyi.ox.ac.uk/dawkins/WorldOfDawkins-archive/Catalano/quotes.shtm 6.9: Stephen Hawking, A Brief History of Time (1992) reprinted by kind permission of The Random House Group Ltd. Scripture quotations taken from the Holy Bible, New International Version, Copyright © 1978, 1984 by International Bible Society. Used by permission of Hodder & Stoughton, a division of Hodder Headline Ltd. All rights reserved. "NIV" is a registered trademark of International Bible Society. UK trademark number 1448790

Contents

Nelson Thornes has worked in partnership with AQA to make sure that this book offers you the best possible support for your GCSE course. All the content has been approved by the senior examining team at AQA, so you can be sure that it gives you just what you need when you are preparing for your exams.

■ How to use this book

This book covers everything you need for your course.

Learning Objectives

At the beginning of each section or topic you'll find a list of Learning Objectives based on the requirements of the specification, so you can make sure you are covering everything you need to know for the exam.

> **Objectives**
>
> **Objectives**
>
> **Objectives**
>
> **Objectives**
>
> First objective.
>
> Second objective.

AQA Examiner's Tips

Don't forget to look at the AQA Examiner's Tips throughout the book to help you with your study and prepare for your exam.

> **AQA Examiner's tip**
>
> Don't forget to look at the AQA Examiner's Tips throughout the book to help you with your study and prepare for your exam.

AQA Examination-style Questions

These offer opportunities to practise doing questions in the style that you can expect in your exam so that you can be fully prepared on the day.

AQA examination questions are reproduced by permission of the Assessment and Qualifications Alliance.

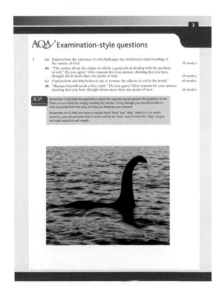

This book is written specifically for GCSE students studying the AQA Religious Studies Specification B, *Unit 4: Religious Philosophy and Ultimate Questions*. Religious philosophy is the study of how religions seek to answer ultimate or 'big' questions such as 'Does God exist?' 'What is God like?' and 'What happens when we die?'

You do not have to be religious to study this course. You simply need to be interested in discussing philosophical questions and finding out what other people think, as well as thinking about your own opinions on questions about the meaning and purpose of life. The unit provides you with the opportunity to develop your knowledge, skills and understanding of religion by exploring philosophical religious questions that challenge believers and non-believers.

■ Topics in this unit

In the examination you will be asked to answer four questions, based on four of the following six topics.

The existence of God

This topic examines the different arguments for the existence of God put forward by believers and the reasons why non-believers reject these arguments.

Revelation

This topic examines the different ways in which God is believed to have revealed himself to believers and what is learned about God through these revelations.

The problems of evil and suffering

This topic considers the problems that the existence of evil and suffering cause for believers, and how believers account for the existence of evil and suffering in a world that they believe is created by God.

Immortality

This topic considers the possibility of life after death. It discusses the different religious and non-religious views on life after death, as well as evidence for and against the possibility of an afterlife.

Miracles

This topic considers the different religious and non-religious views about the concept of miracles, as well as evidence for and against their possibility, particularly the views of the philosopher David Hume.

Science and religion

This topic looks at scientific and religious approaches to two ultimate questions: the origins of the universe and the origins of life.

■ Assessment guidance

The questions set in the examination will allow you to refer in your answers to the religion(s) you have studied. You have to answer four structured essay questions from the choice of six given. Each question is worth 18 marks.

To encourage you to practise the type of question that will be set, each chapter has an assessment guidance section at the end. It will help you to write better answers yourself, if you understand what the examiners are looking for when they mark these questions. To assist you in this, you will be asked to mark an example for yourself – using the mark scheme below. Make sure that you understand the differences between the standard of answer for each level, and what you need to do to achieve full marks.

Examination questions will test two assessment objectives:

AO1	Describe, explain and analyse, using knowledge and understanding.	50%
AO2	Use evidence and reasoned argument to express and evaluate personal responses, informed insights, and differing viewpoints.	50%

The examiner will also take into account the quality of your written communication – how clearly you express yourself and how well you communicate your meaning. The grid below also gives you some guidance on the sort of quality examiners expect to see at different levels.

Levels of response mark scheme for six-mark evaluation questions

Levels	Criteria for AO1	Criteria for AO2	Quality of written communication	Marks
0	Nothing relevant or worthy of credit	An unsupported opinion or no relevant evaluation	The candidate's presentation, spelling, punctuation and grammar seriously obstruct understanding	0 marks
Level 1	Something relevant or worthy of credit	An opinion supported by simple reason	The candidate presents some relevant information in a simple form. The text produced is usually legible. Spelling, punctuation and grammar allow meaning to be derived, although errors are sometimes obstructive	1 mark
Level 2	Elementary knowledge and understanding, e.g. two simple points	An opinion supported by one developed reason or two simple reasons		2 marks
Level 3	Sound knowledge and understanding	An opinion supported by one well developed reason or several simple reasons. N.B. Candidates who make no religious comment should not achieve more than Level 3	The candidate presents relevant information in a way which assists with the communication of meaning. The text produced is legible. Spelling, punctuation and grammar are sufficiently accurate not to obscure meaning	3 marks
Level 4	A clear knowledge and understanding with some development	An opinion supported by two developed reasons with reference to religion		4 marks
Level 5	A detailed answer with some analysis, as appropriate	Evidence of reasoned consideration of two different points of view, showing informed insights and knowledge and understanding of religion	The candidate presents relevant information coherently, employing structure and style to render meaning clear. The text produced is legible. Spelling, punctuation and grammar are sufficiently accurate to render meaning clear	5 marks
Level 6	A full and coherent answer showing good analysis, as appropriate	A well-argued response, with evidence of reasoned consideration of two different points of view showing informed insights and ability to apply knowledge and understanding of religion effectively		6 marks

Note: In evaluation answers to questions worth only 3 marks, the first three levels apply. Questions which are marked out of 3 marks do not ask for two views, but reasons for your own opinion.

Successful study of this unit will result in a Short Course GCSE award. Study of one further unit will provide a Full Course GCSE award. Other units in Specification B which may be taken to achieve a Full Course GCSE award are:

- Unit 1 Religion and Citizenship
- Unit 2 Religion and Life Issues
- Unit 3 Religion and Morality
- Unit 5 Religious Expression in Society
- Unit 6 Worship and Key Beliefs

1.1 How do we prove that things exist?

Research activity 🔍

How René Descartes proved that God existed

René Descartes was a philosopher who lived in France in the 17th century. Descartes believed that he had found a solution to the problem of how to prove God's existence. Use the internet and/or a library to find out how he solved the problem. Share your findings with the rest of the class.

Objectives

Consider how things are proved to exist.

How do we prove that things exist?

There are **three** main ways by which the existence of things is proved:

1 Personal experience – 'I have seen it, so I know it exists.'

2 Reliable evidence – 'I have not seen it but other people have convinced me that they have, so I accept its existence.'

3 Using a chain of reasoning to reach a conclusion (logic) – 'I have not seen it but there must be a logical reason to believe in its existence.'

Does the Loch Ness monster exist?

These three types of evidence can be demonstrated by looking at how people try to prove the existence of the Loch Ness monster. People who accept that Nessie exists use one or all of the following types of proof:

A *René Descartes was born in France in 1596*

- They are certain Nessie exists because they have seen the monster for themselves.

- They accept the accounts and evidence of sightings of Nessie given by other people.

- With all the sightings of Nessie in Loch Ness, it seems more likely that there is a 'monster' in Loch Ness rather than no monster, so it is logical to accept that there is such a creature as Nessie living in Loch Ness.

Other people refuse to accept the evidence people give to prove things. For example, people reject the existence of Nessie because:

- They have not seen any evidence for themselves, so do not accept that Nessie exists.

- They do not accept the evidence of sightings by other people as sufficient proof. They think that the people who claim to have seen Nessie might be hallucinating or lying, or that the sighting is wishful thinking as people want to see the 'monster'. It might be a case of mistaken identity, or a deliberate hoax to fool people.

B *Is this the Loch Ness monster or trick photography?*

- They think that without any proof of such a large creature living in the loch, it is not logical to accept the existence of Nessie.

How do we prove that God exists?

The same types of evidence that are used to prove or reject the existence of Nessie can be used to prove or reject the existence of God. A **theist** is certain that God exists because they:

- are certain that they have been in contact with God directly
- accept the accounts that other people have given of their experience of God as evidence that God exists
- believe that God is the only logical explanation for the origin of the universe and the order within it.

An **atheist** rejects any belief in God, as they do not believe that any evidence accepted by theists is sufficient proof that God exists.

An **agnostic** believes that any evidence produced by theists does not prove the existence of God one way or the other. They believe that it cannot be known whether or not God exists.

Is it important to prove that God exists?

In many ways, the arguments we are going to look at in this chapter are not really proving that God exists, as theists are already sure that God exists, and atheists are unlikely to change their mind unless they have a religious experience. An agnostic will probably think that the arguments do not provide sufficient proof to convince them of God's existence with certainty. Buddhists do not believe in God so any proof offered is not going to change their beliefs.

Key terms

Theist: a person who believes in God.

Atheist: a person who believes there is no God.

Agnostic: a person who believes we cannot be sure whether God exists.

Discussion activity

Divide the class into four groups. Each group represents **one** of the following people:

- a theist who attends a place of worship regularly
- a person who believes in God but does not attend a place of worship
- an atheist
- an agnostic.

Each group is to work out reasons the person would give for their beliefs. Try to support your group's points with evidence.

A representative from each group comes to the front of the class to form part of a *Question Time* panel to discuss whether or not God exists. There needs to be a chairperson to control the discussion. Each member of the panel is to state their views. Then, members of the class can ask the panel questions about their beliefs or add additional points to support or reject a view expressed by the panel.

Activities

'I know that God exists because my prayers have been answered.'

1   Is this statement more likely to be made by an atheist or a theist? Explain your choice.

2   Explain what the term 'agnostic' means.

AQA Examiner's tip

Make sure that you are able to answer questions that ask you what is meant by a 'theist', an 'atheist' and an 'agnostic'.

Summary

You should now be able to explain the evidence theists use to support their belief in the existence of God, and why atheists and agnostics do not accept such evidence as proof for the existence of God.

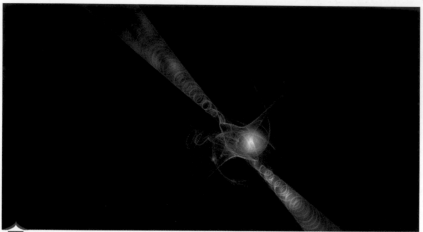

The First Cause argument

Some theists would use the existence of the universe to prove the existence of God. They would argue that:

- Everything that exists was caused to exist.
- The universe exists, so it too must have a cause.
- There had to be something eternal (without beginning or end) that was not caused by anything.
- The eternal first cause is God.
- Therefore God exists.

This is called the First Cause argument. It is given this name because it is arguing that the first cause of the universe is God. The First Cause argument is also known as the **cosmological** argument. The First Cause or cosmological argument tries to prove that there is a perfect and well-ordered universe, and a world in which we live (cosmos), rather than nothingness, because God brought the cosmos into existence. Theists argue that the universe is perfect because it was created by God and is not the result of random chance.

We are able to trace a series of events back in time. For example, you can trace the events of your life back to the moment of your birth, you can continue back to when your parents met and so on. When we follow this series of events back in time, there are two possibilities: either there is a starting point when the universe began and set everything going, or there is no starting point and the universe does not have a beginning. The universe goes back into infinity.

A theist would accept the first possibility that the universe had a beginning. The start of the chain of events that has led to the present time was caused by something outside the universe, and this was God. Some theists argue that if there was not a beginning to the universe, then there would be no adequate explanation for the existence of the universe and all that is in it.

∞ links

Look back to page 9 to be sure that you know the meanings of the terms 'theist', 'atheist' and 'agnostic'.

Key terms

Cosmological: referring to the origin and structure of the universe.

Creation: the act by which God brought the universe into being.

St Thomas Aquinas's First Cause argument

St Thomas Aquinas was a Christian who lived in the Middle Ages. Aquinas believed that the universe had a beginning. He argued that, as things cannot cause themselves to come into existence, then the universe must have been caused to exist by something outside the universe. Aquinas argued that this first cause of the universe was God. If God had not caused the universe to begin, then there would be no universe and therefore we would not exist. As we can see for ourselves that the universe exists, then it must have had a creator to begin it, and that creator is God.

First Cause argument and time

Some people use the fact that we are able to measure time as evidence that the universe had a beginning, because to measure time we need a starting point. A theist would argue that the measurement of time is evidence that the universe had a beginning and that this beginning was caused by God.

B   *St Thomas Aquinas (1225–1274)*

Many Christians believe that the First Cause (cosmological) argument is supported by the **creation** account in Genesis 1:1–3. The Genesis account states that before the universe was created only God existed and at God's command the process of creation began.

In the beginning God created the heavens and the earth.

Now the earth was formless and empty, darkness was over the surface of the deep, and the Spirit of God was hovering over the waters.

And God said, 'Let there be light,' and there was light.

Genesis 1:1–3

1   Read Genesis 1 and 2:1–3 (The Days of Creation). Make notes on what happened at each stage of creation.

C   *There are several creation stories in Hinduism. Here Vishnu appears, resting on the great serpent ANATA, floating on the cosmic ocean.*

With a partner, in a small group or as a whole class, discuss the following statement: 'The existence of the universe proves that God exists.' Do you agree? Give reasons for your answer, showing that you have thought about more than one point of view.

2   Explain the First Cause (cosmological) argument for the existence of God.

3   'The First Cause argument is supported by creation stories.' Do you agree? Give reasons for your answer, showing that you have thought about more than one point of view. Support your answer with reference to religious creation stories.

Using the internet and/or a library, find out more about St Thomas Aquinas's cosmological argument.

You should now be able to explain the First Cause argument, and discuss why some people think that the argument proves that God exists.

The Design argument

Activity

1 Try to imagine that you do not know the purpose of a watch. Look at the stone and the watch in the picture, and write down the differences between them. What would you be able to tell about the watch, even if you did not know what it was used for? How is the watch different from the stone?

Share your thoughts with the rest of the class.

Objectives

Examine the Design argument.

A *What is the difference between a watch and a stone?*

B *Are the heavenly bodies kept in place by God?*

The Design argument

The Design argument states that the universe is too ordered and complicated to have come about by random chance; therefore, it must have been designed. A design needs a designer. The designer of the universe is God. Most Christians believe that the Genesis account of creation supports the Design argument as it shows that God planned the development of the world. The Design argument is sometimes called the **teleological argument**, from the Greek word *teleos* meaning that there is an end or purpose to everything.

Key terms

Teleological argument: the argument that God designed (made) the universe because everything is so intricately made in its detail that it could not have happened by chance.

Discussion activity

With a partner, in a small group or as a whole class, discuss the following statement: 'The disasters that happen in the world prove that it is not designed.' Do you agree? Give reasons for your answer, showing that you have thought about more than one point of view. Remember to think about religious views as well as non-religious views.

St Thomas Aquinas's Design argument

St Thomas Aquinas said that things could only be kept in regular order by an intelligent being. Aquinas said that the planets, sun, moon and stars rotate in the universe in a set pattern because God keeps them in their place.

William Paley's Design argument

William Paley, an 18th-century English philosopher, used the Design (teleological) argument to prove the existence of God. Paley argued that if we found a watch, even if we did not know its function, we would know that there is evidence of design as the parts have been put together for a purpose. In the same way, if we look at the natural world, we can tell that there is evidence of design. Paley used the example of things that are just right for their purpose, such as the eye for sight, birds' wings for flight, and fish gills for breathing under water. He argued that things that are designed need a designer. The designer of the world he believed was God.

When Isaac Newton discovered the existence of gravity, religious believers such as William Paley saw this as part of God's design to keep the regular movement of the heavenly bodies in the universe.

Isaac Newton's Design argument

Isaac Newton used the fact that we have opposable thumbs as evidence of design. Thumbs are called opposable because they can be moved around to touch the other fingers, which give people the ability to grasp things. The way in which the thumb can be used to grasp things is a movement only found in humans and primates, and this is regarded by theists as evidence of God's design.

Also, the fact that we all have individual patterns on our thumbs was regarded by Newton as evidence that God has planned each human separately. Sir Isaac Newton felt that the thumbs were sufficient evidence on their own to prove that God exists, and said, 'In the absence of any other proof, the thumb alone would convince me of God's existence.'

The Anthropic Principle

The Anthropic Principle is a modern version of the Design argument developed in the 1930s by F.R. Tennant. Tennant argued that God planned (designed) the world so that everything was just right for human life to develop. The gravitational force at the moment when the universe began was just right for the universe to come into existence. If the force had been greater, the stars would have been too hot and would have burned out before the universe developed. If the force had been smaller, then the stars would have been too cool and would not have formed. As the universe expanded, it was at the correct rate to allow for the development of galaxies and eventually planets such as the earth. Once the earth formed, it had all the conditions for intelligent life to develop. Theists believe that this fine tuning cannot be chance but the deliberate action of God.

> **AQA / Examiner's tip**
>
> Make sure that you understand what is meant by the Design (teleological) argument and are able to explain it.

> **Activities**
>
> 2   How would a theist explain the Design (teleological) argument for the existence of God to an atheist?
>
> 3   'The Design argument proves that God exists.' Do you agree? Give reasons for your answer, showing that you have thought about more than one point of view.

> **Summary**
>
> You should now be able to explain and discuss the Design argument.

1.4 Do the First Cause and Design arguments prove that God exists?

The basic problem: First Cause argument

The basic problem with the First Cause argument is that it depends on the universe having a beginning, and it is possible that the universe is infinite. Even if we are able to prove that the universe had a beginning, we cannot prove that it was God who caused it to happen.

Research activity

1 **The Big Bang theory**

Using the internet and/or a library, research the Big Bang theory and write an account of it.

The Big Bang theory

Most scientists would accept that the universe came into existence through the **Big Bang** theory.

Atheists often use the Big Bang theory to reject the existence of God. They argue that it proves that the universe resulted from a random spontaneous event, not an action by God, and that religious accounts of creation are just myths.

Many theists use the Big Bang theory to support the First Cause argument and say that it describes how God caused the universe to exist. Islam accepts that scientific findings support God's existence and creation of the universe.

The Big Bang theory is a challenge to the First Cause argument only if it is thought to be a spontaneous random event without reason or cause. On the other hand, if it is accepted that there must be a reason why the Big Bang happened, a cause, then there is no reason why that cause could not be God.

A challenge to the First Cause argument

The First Cause argument states that things exist because they are caused to exist, and this includes the universe which was caused by God, who is eternal. Atheists and agnostics challenge the argument by saying that it contradicts itself. If the argument is that things exist because they are caused to exist, then what caused God? If God is eternal, then why cannot the universe be eternal?

Theists reply that the argument only applies to God as only God is outside time and space and eternal. As scientists do not know what caused the Big Bang, then why could it not be God?

The basic problem: Design argument

The basic problem with the Design argument is that it depends on the belief that everything in the world is designed, and the designer is God. Not everyone believes that humans are the result of design and,

Objectives

Examine the basic problems with the First Cause and Design arguments.

Explore how strong these arguments are to prove the existence of God, and the weaknesses that lie within them.

Key terms

Big Bang: the beginnings of the universe according to many scientists took place when a singularity exploded and from this explosion, all the matter that makes up the universe came into being.

Evolution: scientific belief that life forms have changed over time, developing from simple to complex creatures.

∞ links

Look back to pages 10–11 for evidence that theists would use to prove that the universe is not infinite.

even if the world is designed, we cannot prove that the designer is God. The design may be the work of many gods or an apprentice god.

The theory of evolution

Many atheists use Darwin's theory of **evolution** to account for apparent design in the world. Atheists would argue that it is through evolution that features such as the opposable thumb developed and not design by God. Atheists such as the zoologist Richard Dawkins argue that it is evolution that has given the appearance of design, not God.

A   *Is the ability to paint necessary for survival?*

Some theists argue that if humans had evolved through natural selection, then they would not need to write books, paint pictures or create music to survive. The fact that humans can do these things suggests that we are designed and, for a theist, this designer is God.

Research activity

2   **The theory of evolution**

Using the internet and/or a library, research the theory of evolution and write an account of it.

Extension activities

Richard Dawkins argues that the variations in the world are caused by random mutations in the DNA molecules of any life form, which leads to the guided process of natural selection. He does not, however, believe that the process is guided by God.

1   Using the internet and/or a library, find out more about Richard Dawkins' views.

2   Use your research to explain why Richard Dawkins wrote a book called *The Blind Watchmaker*.

AQA   *Examiner's tip*

You need to be able to explain not only the challenges an atheist would make to a belief in the existence of God, but also the response a theist would give to these challenges.

A challenge to the Design argument

Atheists point to the existence of the cruelty and suffering found within nature as evidence that the world is not designed – a designer would not have included such flaws.

Theists reply that God is beyond human understanding and there will be an explanation for natural evil and suffering which human beings do not yet understand, or perhaps will never understand.

Discussion activity

Scientific theories, such as the Big Bang theory and the theory of evolution, have provided atheists with reasons why the universe exists and how human life has evolved without having to accept that it is the work of God.

Theists point to the world around us and argue that we are here in a well-ordered universe that is just right to support life. This can only be the work of God and not a random chance event.

With a partner or in a small group, discuss whether you agree with the atheist or the theist. Give reasons for your answer, showing that you have thought about more than one point of view.

links

Find out more about the problem of evil and suffering for a theist in Chapter 3, which begins on page 52.

Activities

1   Explain how the Big Bang theory would challenge the First Cause argument.

2   Explain how the theory of evolution would challenge the Design argument.

Summary

You should now be able to discuss the challenges to the First Cause and Design arguments.

Argument from miracles for the existence of God

What is a miracle?

Theists use the term '**miracle**' to refer to an event performed by God that appears to break the laws of nature. It may be the cure of a terminal illness or disability that doctors cannot explain. It may be survival from certain death by a freak event. However, to be a miracle there needs to be some religious significance or purpose to the event; such as the strengthening of faith or the demonstration of God's love.

Objectives

Examine the argument from miracles for the existence of God.

A *Was it a miracle that 16 people survived in stairwell B?*

Key terms

Miracle: a seemingly impossible occurrence, usually good.

Case study

The miracle of stairwell B, 11th September 2001

An event regarded by many people as a miracle occurred when 16 people survived when the North Tower of the World Trade Center collapsed after the terrorist attack on 9/11. They were all trapped on stairwell B. One group of firemen and the woman they were rescuing were buried under half a million tonnes of debris, but amazingly survived to contact the outside world. Eventually, they were rescued and were able to walk out of the wreckage. Another survivor had reached the 22nd floor when the building collapsed and he felt himself falling through space. Two hours later, he regained consciousness on a slab of concrete 180 feet below the 22nd floor and was rescued by the fire service. The fact that these people survived when nearly 3,000 people died is regarded by many people as a miracle. Those who do not believe in miracles suggest that their survival was the result of the fact that they were protected by the stairwell and ended up near the top of the debris. As they could see sunlight after the collapses or were with someone who could, they had hope and this stopped them from giving up.

Types of miracle

There are two types of miracle:

1   Events that break the laws of nature and cannot be explained by the sciences. For example, Jesus is said to have turned water into wine at the marriage in Cana.

2   Events in which no laws of nature are broken but a coincidence occurs at just the right time to cause a good outcome. This is believed to be because of God's intervention. For example, a toddler is trapped on the railway line in the path of an express train. The train driver collapses and the train comes to a halt before it hits the child.

B   *Jesus turns the water into wine at the Wedding in Cana*

Research activity

1   **Jesus turns water into wine**

Read the account of Jesus turning water into wine in John 2:1–8 in the New Testament.

Discussion activity

With a partner, in a small group or as a whole class, discuss what you think is the religious significance or purpose of the miracle of stairwell B or Jesus turning water into wine.

Research activity

2   **Miracles at Lourdes and at the Sikh Golden Temple in Amritsar**

Using the internet and/or a library, find examples of healing miracles that have taken place at Lourdes, and miracles that have occurred at the Golden Temple.

AQA   Examiner's tip

Make sure that you have examples of the two types of miracle so you can use them to support your answers in the examination.

Extension activity

Using the internet and/or a library, find more examples of incidents that people have believed to be miracles.

Argument from miracles

Theists use the argument from miracles to prove the existence of God by arguing that, as there is no natural explanation for what happened, then it must be a supernatural event. The miracle must have been caused by something outside nature and, as only God is outside nature, then it must be the result of God's intervention in the world. Therefore, God exists.

Activities

1   Explain the term 'miracle'.

2   Explain the **two** different types of miracle.

3   'Miracles do not prove the existence of God.' Do you agree? Give reasons for your answer, showing that you have thought about more than one point of view.

Summary

You should now be able to discuss the argument from miracles for the existence of God.

Argument from religious experience for the existence of God

What is meant by a religious experience?

Some theists are certain that God exists because they claim to have experienced God. When people claim to have met God personally, this is called a **religious experience** and it can take many forms. A religious experience can occur to either an individual or a group of people. Religious experiences that believers may claim to have had include:

- communicating with God through prayer and meditation
- feeling God's presence in worship
- feeling the presence of God in nature
- experiencing a conversion
- involvement in a miraculous event.

Communicating with God through prayer and meditation

Through prayer, believers are not only speaking to God, but are also listening for God's reply. During such times, believers say that they have felt the presence of God and are in no doubt of God's existence. Some worshippers use meditation to feel closer to God. Others will withdraw from everyday life and 'go on retreat' to give their full attention to God.

Feeling God's presence in worship

Believers may feel God's presence in worship. For Christians, this might be a charismatic event, which is worship based on the belief that during a service it is possible to receive the gifts of the Holy Spirit. This may also occur in a sacrament, which is worship such as Holy Communion where it is believed that there is an outward sign of an inner gift from God.

Objectives

Examine the argument from religious experience for the existence of God.

Key terms

Religious experience: an experience that is outside normal experience, usually involving the supernatural.

⚭ links

Look back to pages 16–17 to remind yourself of how a theist argues that miracles prove God exists.

Case study

Pentecostal worship

Pentecostal worship is an example of Christian worship in which there may be a charismatic event. Pentecostalists believe that the gifts of the Holy Spirit are available to the faithful and it is through these gifts that they experience God. Sometimes members of the congregation may feel overwhelmed by God's Holy Spirit, and they almost faint and fall on the floor. Other members of the congregation may 'speak in tongues' as they feel so moved by the Holy Spirit that normal speech seems inadequate. To outsiders, it sounds like a jumble of sounds, but other members of the Church translate the sounds for the rest of the congregation. Other worshippers believe that they have the gift of prophecy and can 'hear' God's voice and say what it means. Sometimes members of the Church appear to have the gift of healing and use these gifts to try to cure people of illness in faith healing services.

A *Pentecostalists feel moved by the Holy Spirit*

Catholic Mass

The Catholic Church is a Christian tradition that celebrates the sacramental ritual of Holy Communion. They call this service the Mass. Catholics believe that when the priest consecrates the bread and wine, it becomes the actual body and blood of Christ. These Christians believe that during the Mass, Christ's sacrifice for the forgiveness of sins is repeated. The bread and wine are believed to be food and drink for the spiritual life of those taking part in the service, to gain eternal life and God's forgiveness.

B *Some people feel the presence of God through the beauty of nature*

Feeling the presence of God in nature

Some believers are convinced that they have felt the presence of God while walking in the countryside because of feelings of awe and wonder they experience while looking at the beauty of nature.

Experiencing a conversion

Some theists believe that God has contacted them directly and, as a result, experience a conversion. They may be converted to believe in God or to change their beliefs about God. An early Christian, St Paul, was originally a Jew who wanted to kill Christians. On his way to the city of Damascus, he had a religious experience that converted him to Christianity.

Discussion activities

1 Paul was called Saul before his conversion. With a partner, discuss why you think he changed his name when he converted to Christianity.
2 With a partner, discuss the reasons why theists might accept Paul's conversion as genuine, and the reasons that atheists might give for denying it was a religious experience.

Activities

1 Read the account of the conversion of St Paul in Acts 9:1–22.
2 Imagine that you are Ananias and write a letter to the Christians in Jerusalem telling them what has happened.

Research activity

Examples of religious experience

Using the internet and/or a library, research the religious experiences of:
- the Buddha
- Guru Nanak
- Mahatma Ghandi
- Muhammad.

Write an account of each person's religious experience.

Activities

3 What is meant by a 'religious experience'?
4 How might either prayer or meditation help someone to experience God?
5 How might God be experienced through sacramental rituals?
6 What is meant by a 'conversion'?
7 Describe an example of a religious conversion.

Summary

You should now be able to discuss the argument from religious experience for the existence of God.

1.7 Do the arguments from miracles and religious experience prove that God exists?

The basic problem: miracles

The basic problem with the argument from miracles for the existence of God is that miracles are difficult to prove. Atheists and agnostics may argue that miracles are no more than coincidences. For example, they would argue that a parachutist who survived after his parachute did not open did so by chance and not by a miracle. They argue that there are logical reasons for what is claimed to be a miracle other than the intervention of God. The reasons they give for rejecting miracles besides coincidence include the following:

- What appears to be a miracle may be something that science cannot explain yet.
- Theists want miracles to happen, so they give miraculous claims to ordinary events.
- The cure of an illness may be the result of mind over matter and the belief that the sufferer would be cured.
- It may be that the doctors wrongly diagnosed an illness and the person was cured naturally.
- Some 'miracles' are fakes or made up by individuals wanting fame or money.

Is God picking and choosing whom is helped?

Some theists do not believe in miracles as they argue that if they occur, then God is picking and choosing who is helped and this does not seem fair or loving. For example, if it was a miracle that saved 16 people when the North Tower of the World Trade Center collapsed, why did God choose to save only them and to allow thousands to die? Some theists argue that this would mean God does not act fairly as God is picking and choosing who is helped and who is not. As God is not like this, then miracles do not happen.

Other theists would reply that miracles are not for the benefit of individuals but for everyone. Miracles prove the existence of God, and teach people about God. Miraculous healings, for example, might be taken as signs of the existence of a loving God.

Do miracles occur?

Most theists would answer 'yes, miracles do occur', as they would argue that there are too many accounts of miracles for them not to happen, and not all miracles happen to believers. Miracles can convert people to believing in God and this is further evidence that they are genuine.

A further argument in favour of miracles is that miracles are often investigated by religious believers before they are accepted as genuine. For example, six million pilgrims go to Lourdes each year hoping for a

Objectives

Examine the basic problems with the arguments from miracles and religious experience for the existence of God.

Explore how strong these arguments are to prove the existence of God, and the weaknesses that lie within them.

links

Look back to pages 16–17 to remind yourself of what is meant by the argument from miracles for the existence of God.

Look back to pages 18–19 to remind yourself of what is meant by the argument from religious experience for the existence of God.

Extension activity

Using the internet and/or a library, find out why the philosopher David Hume did not believe in miracles.

links

Look back to page 16 to remind yourself of what happened during the miracle of stairwell B.

miracle, but the Roman Catholic Church accepts that only 66 miracles have occurred since the Medical Bureau was established in 1882. The miraculous claims to be cured are checked not only by priests, but also a panel of doctors.

■ The basic problem: religious experience

The main problem in using religious experiences as proof of the existence of God is that they are difficult to prove as genuine. The only evidence for people who have not had the experience themselves is the effect on the individual claiming to have experienced God.

Atheists and agnostics do not accept religious experiences as proof of the existence of God. They believe that people are mistaken or misled. People might have imagined the experience because they wanted to believe that God exists or they might have mistaken an ordinary experience as religious. People may have been under the influence of drugs or alcohol and thought that they had a religious experience or, while ill, had a hallucination that they thought was a real event.

Theists would reply that the influence of religious experiences is so great that they must be genuine. The fact that people have had direct personal proof of the existence of God provides them with clear evidence that God exists. The experience results in people converting to a faith or finding that their faith is strengthened, and this leads to life changes. Some believers are even willing to die for their faith after they have had a religious experience. Sometimes several people share a religious experience, so they cannot all be hallucinating.

A   *Six million pilgrims go to Lourdes each year hoping for a miracle*

Activities

The first person to die for their faith in Islam was a woman, Sumayyah bint Khayyat. She believed so strongly in Islam that she was willing to die for her beliefs.

1 Using the internet and/or a library, find out about her martyrdom.
2 Write an account of her death; include evidence that shows that she kept her faith to the end.

Research activities

1 **The Toronto Blessing**

   Religious experience can occur to a group of people as well as individuals, and this is strong evidence to support the experience as genuine. Using the internet, find out about the experience known as the Toronto Blessing.

2 **A miracle cure at Lourdes**

   Sometimes when one person is miraculously cured, it can affect others who see the event. Using the internet, find out about the conversion of the famous writer and agnostic Alexis Carrel to Catholicism after he saw Marie Bailly cured at Lourdes.

Discussion activity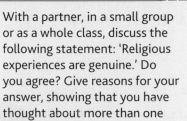

With a partner, in a small group or as a whole class, discuss the following statement: 'Religious experiences are genuine.' Do you agree? Give reasons for your answer, showing that you have thought about more than one point of view.

AQA Examiner's tip

You need to show that you have thought about not only the challenges an atheist would make to an argument from religious experience, but also the response a theist would give to these challenges.

Summary

You should now be able to discuss the challenges to the arguments for the existence of God from miracles and religious experience.

The argument from morality for the existence of God

1 Read the following passage and complete the task that follows.

A woman is diagnosed with cancer and she and her husband are told that she will only live for a few more months. The doctor tells them that there is a new treatment that would cure her cancer but it is only available in certain health authorities and, unfortunately, their authority is not one of them. The man asks, if he moved his wife to one of these health authorities would she get the treatment? The doctor answers that they would have to be resident in the area for at least six months before she would be treated and she is unlikely to live that long. The man writes to the drug company and asks the cost of the drug. The man has given up his job to look after his wife so has a low income and cannot afford the cost quoted by the drug company. The man realises that the company is not far from where he lives and decides to break into the company and steal enough of the drug to cure his wife.

The man has made a moral decision. List all the things that will have guided him in making this moral decision.

Objectives

Examine the argument from morality for the existence of God.

A *Bad news from the drug company*

B *Is it ever right to steal in order to save life?*

Discussion activity

Do you agree with the man's decision to break into the drug company and steal the drugs? Discuss your views with your teacher and the rest of the class.

What is morality?

Morality is a sense of right and wrong that helps guide people's behaviour. A moral action is an action that is believed to be right according to the rules/laws of the society, country or religion in which a person lives. People have to make decisions all the time about what is right or wrong. For some people, it is the consequence of an action that needs to be considered when deciding whether an action is right. For example, in the case of the woman with cancer (see Activity on page 22), would stealing the drugs be morally right if the woman was cured of cancer?

Other people look at the motives of an action to decide whether it is morally right. For example, in the case of the woman with cancer, has the man made the decision to steal the drugs because he loves his wife and wants to relieve her suffering?

The argument from morality for the existence of God

Theists argue that the fact that most people have a powerful sense that they should behave in a moral way is evidence for the existence of God. Some theists would argue that our sense of right and wrong is 'built in' by God. They would argue that:

- People have an inbuilt sense of morality.
- This sense comes from a source outside of them.
- This source is God.
- Therefore God exists.

Morality takes priority

Some theists argue that we do things that are morally right because it is what we think we ought to do, even when we would prefer to act in a different way. For example, my grandmother is very ill and lives in a different town. I have promised my parents I will go with them to visit her on Saturday. I win tickets to see my favourite group playing in concert. I cannot do both. I would prefer to go to the concert, but morally I ought not. I should visit my grandmother as promised. The fact that morality is a command that must be obeyed means that it comes from an ultimate authority and this authority is God, therefore God exists.

Moral behaviour does not always get fair treatment

People argue that morality is a reasonable way to behave; and people who behave morally need to get justice. However, there are people who always behave in a moral way but they do not seem to get a happy life as a result. Some theists argue that moral behavior must be rewarded, so those who do not get fair treatment in this life are rewarded after death. This means that God must exist to raise people to life after death in heaven.

Conscience is the voice of God

Some theists argue that the fact that we have a **conscience** is evidence for the existence of God. Conscience is like an inner voice from God that guides our behaviour; it can make us feel good when we behave well, and guilty or ashamed when we do something we think or know is wrong.

Activities

2 Explain the term 'morality'.
3 Explain the argument from morality for the existence of God.

AQA   Examiner's tip

Make sure that you are able to explain what is meant by the terms 'morality' and 'conscience', and that you can link these terms to the argument from morality for the existence of God.

Summary

You should now be able to discuss the argument from morality for the existence of God.

1.9 Does the argument from morality prove that God exists?

The basic problem: morality

The basic problem with the argument from morality for the existence of God is that it is difficult to prove that morality exists, and that morality is no more than rules or laws developed to control people. Atheists and agnostics claim that morality is part of human development through evolution. They argue that morality is part of the survival process required in a world in which the resources necessary to support life are scarce and danger is all around us. People who cooperate are more likely to survive and reproduce than groups of people who do not. As a result, natural selection has favoured morality because it has survival value.

Theists who accept the theory of evolution would consider that the fact that morality helps people to survive is part of God's design for human development.

Guilt feelings are not from God

Theists argue that conscience is the voice of God guiding them. When they get guilt feelings, then it is God telling them that they have done wrong.

Atheists and agnostics challenge this. They argue that people have guilt feelings because they have gone against the moral rules provided by the society, religion and/or family in which they were raised. If people are brought up to believe that drinking alcohol is wrong, then they will probably get guilt feelings if they drink alcohol. Atheists and agnostics consider guilt feelings to be caused by a conflict between people's desires and the controlling influences of society, religion and/or family.

Also, not everyone feels guilt – even when they do something that most people would consider wrong.

Is moral behaviour rewarded by an afterlife?

Atheists and agnostics ask why behaving in a moral way should guarantee reward. It may be that it is random chance whether or not people have a happy life and it is not linked to the way in which they behave. They would add that, as there is no evidence to support life after death, this cannot be used as evidence to support the argument from morality for the existence of God.

Objectives

Examine the strengths and weaknesses in the argument from morality for the existence of God.

links

Look back to pages 22–23 to remind yourself of what is meant by the argument from morality for the existence of God.

Look back to page 15 to remind yourself of what is meant by evolution.

links

Look back to page 23 to check that you understand what is meant by the term 'conscience'.

Extension activity

Using the internet and/or a library, find out what Sigmund Freud thought was the cause of guilt feelings.

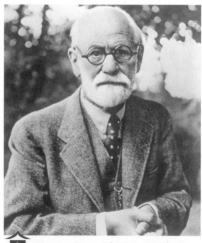

A Sigmund Freud (1856–1939), the founder of psychoanalysis

B *'And have you behaved as God instructed?'*

Theists believe that there is life after death. God has provided moral guidance so that people know how to behave, so that they will be rewarded for their good behaviour after death.

Discussion activity

Organise a class debate to discuss the following statement: 'The fact that people behave in a moral way proves that God exists.'

Activity

'The argument from morality for the existence of God is a strong argument.' Do you agree? Give reasons for your answer, showing that you have thought about more than one point of view.

AQA *Examiner's tip*

You need to show that you have thought about not only the challenges an atheist would make to the argument from morality, but also the response a theist would give to these challenges.

Summary

You should now be able to discuss the challenges to the argument from morality for the existence of God.

Arguments against belief in the existence of God

The importance of faith to belief in God

In this chapter we have looked at the various arguments for the existence of God. These are:

- the First Cause (cosmological) argument
- the Design (teleological) argument
- the argument from miracles
- the argument from religious experience
- the argument from morality.

These arguments are important to theists because they support the **faith** that theists already have in the existence of God. The First Cause argument, the Design argument and the argument from morality do not prove the existence of God to the believer on their own, but they help to strengthen the belief that the theist already has in the existence of God. A religious experience, including a miracle, may prove the existence of God to individuals, and convert an atheist or agnostic into a believer in God. Once people are converted into believing in God, then they have faith.

Atheists do not have faith in God and, therefore, they are going to find alternative explanations for the arguments theists put forward for believing in God. Agnostics would argue that there is still insufficient evidence to prove whether or not God exists.

Using science to deny the existence of God

In the past, the origin of the universe and life on earth could not be explained, and so it was accepted that God created and controlled everything in the universe. When people became sick or the crops failed, it was thought to be a punishment from God for some wrongdoing. People looked to their religion for answers. However, the more science has explained things that people could not understand in the past, the more people have turned away from belief in God. Atheists argue that science is able to provide all the answers and belief in God is no longer needed. Also, because science is now close to actually creating human life, atheists believe that this may be further evidence that God does not exist.

Discussion activity

1 With a partner, in a small group or as a whole class, discuss what you think the reply of a theist would be to the following view: 'Science has all the answers and so God is no longer needed.'

Objectives

Understand why atheists do not believe in the existence of God.

links

Look back to pages 10–25 if you are not sure of any of the arguments for the existence of God mentioned in this section.

Key terms

Faith: a commitment to something that goes beyond proof and knowledge, especially used about God and religion.

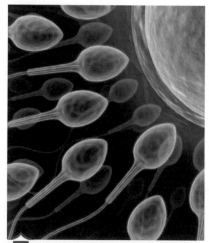

A *Scientists are close to creating human life*

B *Is cruelty in nature evidence that God does not exist?*

The presence of evil and suffering in the world

Atheists point to the existence of evil and suffering in the world as evidence that God does not exist, or is not as powerful or loving as theists believe. They point out that the suffering is often unjust and affects good and innocent people. This topic will be examined in more detail in Chapter 3, but it is important to remember that the existence of evil and suffering is a reason why people argue against God's existence. Their reasons include the following:

- The cruelty in the animal kingdom and the natural disasters that cause suffering are evidence of poor design.
- People do not always behave in a moral way, so they must be able to ignore their conscience. Therefore, conscience cannot be the voice of God.

Theists provide some reasons for the existence of evil and suffering, but will also admit that there are some things beyond human understanding, and they continue to believe in the existence of God. These reasons are explained in Chapter 3.

Discussion activity

2 With a partner, in a small group or as a whole class, discuss the following statement: 'It is hard to prove that God exists.'

Remember to consider all of the arguments for the existence of God, as well as the challenges from atheists and agnostics in your discussion.

AQA Examiner's tip

Remember to describe the problems raised by evil and suffering in your answers to questions about the existence of God.

Activities

1 What is meant by 'faith'?
2 Why do atheists argue that scientific discoveries prove that God does not exist?
3 Why do atheists argue that the existence of evil and suffering in the world proves that God does not exist?
4 'God cannot be proved to exist.' Do you agree? Give reasons for your answer, showing that you have thought about more than one point of view.

Summary

You should now be able to discuss the arguments against the existence of God.

1

The existence of God – summary

For the examination you should now be able to:

✔ explain the terms 'theist', 'atheist' and 'agnostic'

✔ outline the following arguments theists use to prove the existence of God:
- First Cause (cosmological) argument
- Design (teleological) argument
- argument from miracles
- argument from religious experience
- argument from morality

✔ outline the arguments used by atheists and agnostics against belief in God

✔ give reasons for and against these arguments as proof of the existence of God.

Sample answer

1 Write an answer to the following examination question:

'The Big Bang theory proves that there is no God.' Do you agree? Give reasons for your answer, showing you have thought about more than one point of view. Refer to religious arguments in your answer. *(6 marks)*

2 Read the following sample answer:

> I think that the existence of God cannot be proved or disproved by science or religion, so the statement is false. However, I can see why some people say that the Big Bang theory proves there is no God. Some scientists say that the Big Bang did not need a 'God' to start it off. It just happened by random chance. Just because the universe had a beginning does not mean it had a divine cause.
>
> Some theists might disagree with me. They would say that scientists do not really know why the Big Bang started, and therefore the cause could be God. There is no proof that it was not God. Scientists do not have all the answers about the Big Bang. It is just a theory. Many religious people believe both in God and the Big Bang. They say that science shows how God brought the universe into existence.

3 With a partner, discuss the sample answer. Do you think that there are other things that the student could have included in the answer?

4 What mark would you give this answer out of 6? (Look at the mark scheme in the Introduction on page 7 (AO2) before you attempt this.) What are the reasons for the mark you have given?

AQA Examination-style questions

1 Look at the drawings and answer the following questions.

I do not believe that God exists because people make each other suffer.

I believe God caused the Big Bang.

I am not sure if the world is designed or not.

(a) (i) Which statement was made by a theist? *(1 mark)*
(ii) Which statement was made by an atheist? *(1 mark)*

(b) Explain an argument from religious experience for the existence of God. *(4 marks)*

(c) 'Miracles prove that God exists.' What do you think? Explain your opinion. *(3 marks)*

(d) Explain briefly the reasons some people might give for believing that the world was not designed by God. *(3 marks)*

(e) 'People behave in a moral way because God exists.' Do you agree? Give reasons for your answer, showing that you have thought about more than one point of view. Refer to religious arguments in your answer. *(6 marks)*

 Examiner's tip Remember that when you are given a statement and asked 'do you agree?' you must show what you think and the reasons why other people might take a different view. If your answer is one sided, you can only achieve a maximum of 4 marks. If you make no comment about religious belief or practice, you will achieve no more than 3 marks.

2.1 What is meant by revelation?

What is a revelation?

For a religious believer a **revelation** occurs when something about God, the way in which God wants people to behave, or the meaning of life becomes clear or visible. Buddhists do not believe in God and so, for them, revelation is a revelation that leads to an understanding of the nature of things.

For theists, revelation is believed to come directly from God, or may be brought indirectly by an angel or some other means. Each religion, with the exception of Hinduism, is founded on the revelations received by the founders of the faith, which are then preserved in the religion's sacred writings.

Objectives

Investigate what is meant by revelation.

Investigate ideas of how God is revealed to humans.

⬭ links

Look back to page 9 to remind yourself of the meaning of the terms 'theist', 'atheist' and 'agnostic'.

Research activity

Founders of religion

Choose **two** of the following founders of religion and find out how each founder received revelations:

- The Buddha (Buddhism)
- Jesus (Christianity)
- Muhammad (Islam)
- Abraham or Moses (Judaism)
- Guru Nanak (Sikhism)

Beliefs and teachings

God and revelation

It is not fitting for a man that Allah should speak to him except by inspiration, or from behind a veil, or by the sending of a Messenger to reveal, with Allah's permission, what Allah wills: for He is Most High, Most Wise. And thus have We, by Our command, sent inspiration to thee: thou knewest not (before) what was Revelation, and What was Faith; but We have made the (Qur'an) a Light, wherewith We guide such of Our servants as We will...

Qur'an 42:51–52

A *God first revealed himself to Moses through a burning bush*

B *Some people believe that revelation comes through the beauty of the natural world*

How does God reveal himself?

The first question to ask is whether or not God can be known. Some theists would argue that God cannot be known because God is beyond human understanding and cannot be described using the limits of human language.

Many religious believers think that it is possible to understand certain qualities of God but only if God himself makes them known through revelations. People, therefore, receive revelations when God chooses to reveal himself. It is thought that God reveals himself in many different ways. The ways in which God reveals himself are through:

- a direct meeting, dream or vision
- nature
- worship
- prayer
- sacred writings
- people
- miracles
- conscience
- belief (conviction).

Christian beliefs about God

To describe God as having both **immanence** and **transcendence** seems to be describing opposing ways of describing God's nature. Most Christians believe that God is beyond people's understanding, and outside time and space, and that God's power is unlimited. This is why Christians say that they believe in an Almighty God. Although God is believed to be transcendent, most Christians believe God is also immanent because God has been, is and will be involved in the history of the world. Christians believe that God became immanent in the form of Jesus, to show people how he wanted them to live according to his will. God remains immanent through the action of the Holy Spirit. It is an important part of Christianity that God is both transcendent and immanent.

Case study

General revelation and special revelation

There are two main kinds of revelation through which theists believe God may be known: **general revelation** and **special revelation**. The next two sections look at the differences between these two kinds of revelation.

Discussion activity ■■■

Read the extract from the Qur'an 42:51–52 on page 30. Discuss with a partner what this teaches about Allah and revelation.

Key terms

Revelation: God shows himself to believers. This is the only way anybody can really know anything about God.

Immanence: the idea that God is present in and involved with life on earth and in the universe (a quality of God).

Transcendence: the idea that God is beyond and outside life on earth and the universe (a quality of God).

Activities

❝ *I know that God exists because my prayers have been answered.* ❞

1 Explain what a religious believer means by a 'revelation'.
2 Why do theists believe that it is not possible to know God?
3 Explain **three** ways in which God may reveal himself.

Summary

You should now be able to discuss what is meant by revelation.

2.2 General revelation

What is general revelation?

General revelation is God becoming known through ordinary, common, human experiences or natural means. General revelation is indirect and available to everyone. The ways in which general revelations come to people include:

- seeing the presence of God in nature
- seeing God in the holy book(s) of the religion
- seeing God in the writings of religious leaders
- seeing God in the life and work of other people
- seeing God's character revealed through reason, conscience and faith
- experiencing God through prayer and worship.

A *Does the power of nature reveal anything about God?*

Seeing the presence of God in nature

The beauty and power of nature, the complexity of the human body and the creation of new life are thought by many religious believers to be evidence that God is immanent in the world. This leads to feelings of awe and wonder at the power of God to create and to destroy.

Seeing God in the holy book(s) of the religion

A major way in which God is believed to be revealed is through the scriptures (holy books) of the religion. For some religions, such as Islam, the holy book (the Qur'an) is believed to be the actual words of Allah revealed directly to the Prophet Muhammad. For other believers, the words of their holy book are inspired by God but not revealed by God directly. When believers listen to the words from the holy book or read it for themselves, they hope to get a better understanding of the teachings of the religion and to receive spiritual strength from God's words.

Objectives

Investigate what is meant by general revelation.

Explore examples of general revelation.

Understand how these examples can act as a revelation.

Key terms

General revelation: God making himself known through ordinary, common human experiences.

AQA Examiner's tip

You need to be able to explain the differences between general and special revelation.

Activity

1 One form of general revelation is seeing the presence of God in nature.

Look back at the Design argument on pages 11–12 and the argument from religious experience found in nature on page 19. Write a paragraph to explain how the natural world might act as a general revelation.

∞ links

Look back to page 31 to remind yourself of the difference in meaning of immanence and transcendence.

Extension activity

1 Using the internet and/or a library, find out more about how Jews believe God is revealed through the Torah.

Seeing God in the writings of religious leaders

The writings of religious leaders help believers to understand the nature of God. Some religious leaders, past and present, write explanations of the sacred texts of the religion to help followers understand what sacred texts reveal about God, or they may publish reports on how believers should live their lives according to the will of God.

Case study

An example of religious writing

The Pope is the head of the Roman Catholic Church, and gives guidance to Catholics on matters of faith and morality through statements called encyclicals. A famous encyclical called *Humanae Vitae* (On Human Life) was issued by Pope Paul VI in 1968. This encyclical stated the traditional Catholic teaching about the use of birth control, and still influences the lives of Catholics today. *Humanae Vitae* is an important source of moral authority for Catholics.

Seeing God in the life and work of other people

The way someone has behaved in their life and work is sometimes so extraordinary that religious believers feel that God has guided them. By studying the life and work of these individuals, religious believers think that they can find out more about God.

There are many examples in the different religions of how some people's lives have inspired others to believe in God or to behave better in their lives. The life and work of these religious people give an example to others that God exists and show how God wants them to behave. This is especially true when people have been willing to die for their beliefs.

Seeing God's character revealed through reason, conscience and faith

Some theists believe that our ability to **reason** tells us about God. Other believers would argue that the fact that we have a **conscience** and feel guilty when we have done wrong is evidence of the existence of God. For others, the desire to worship God is evidence in itself of God. They are certain that God exists and that this faith is all they need.

Experiencing God through prayer and worship

Prayer and worship can be both general and special revelation according to whether or not God has made himself known directly or indirectly. Some people may feel the direct presence of God during acts of worship, and this is special revelation. For others, their desire to take part in acts of worship is general revelation.

B *The Dalai Lama provides an example to others*

Activities

2 Explain what is meant by a 'general revelation'.

3 Explain **three** examples of general revelation.

4 'An immanent God is better than a transcendent one.' Do you agree? Give reasons for your answer, showing that you have thought about more than one point of view.

Summary

You should now be able to discuss what is meant by a general revelation.

Special revelation

What is special revelation?

Special revelation occurs when God is believed to have spoken directly to an individual or a group of people. It is different from general revelation because it is not a general everyday experience that is there for everyone to see and believe in. It is 'specially' for one person or a group of people. The ways in which special revelations come to people include:

- enlightenment
- hearing God's call
- experiencing **visions** or dreams
- through miracles
- through prayer and worship.

Enlightenment

Buddhists do not believe in God and seek understanding of what is true and what is not (enlightenment). Buddhists are seeking how to end suffering and achieve happiness by escaping the cycle of birth and death.

Hearing God's call

The founders of the religions we are studying, as well as other religious people, believe that God has spoken to them directly – a special revelation. The message received may result in the individual changing their way of life or beliefs. They may experience a conversion. This, in itself, is seen by many people as evidence that God has spoken to them. The message that the person receives is then shared with other believers and becomes a general revelation.

Experiencing visions or dreams

Religious believers, who believe that they have heard the voice of God, often hear that voice in visions and dreams.

Visions are one form of special revelation in which people see holy people, angels or hear messages from God. An example of a Christian who received visions was St Bernadette. She saw visions of the Virgin Mary and was told that the waters of Lourdes had healing properties.

A *Buddhists seek enlightenment by following the example of the Buddha*

Dreams are another way by which people believe that they have had a direct (special) revelation from God. An example of a dream as special revelation is found in the story of Jacob (Genesis 28:10–22). When he saw a ladder to heaven and angels going up and down it, he realised that God is willing to forgive sins if people turn back to God.

Beliefs and teachings

God says that he will reveal himself in visions and dreams

> He said, 'Listen to my words:
> When a prophet of the LORD is among you,
> I reveal myself to him in visions,
> I speak to him in dreams.'

Numbers 12:6

Revelation through miracles

Miraculous healing is when a person recovers from a serious illness or disability in a way that medical science cannot explain. An amazing recovery like this often convinces people that God has intervened. Christians say that there have been many cases of miraculous healing at Lourdes, for example, and many Hindus believe that the river Ganges has healing properties.

B   *People believe that they have direct contact with God through prayer*

Revelation through prayer and worship

Prayer and worship are examples of special revelation when the worshipper believes that God has communicated with them directly during the act of prayer or worship. We will look more at the impact of prayer and worship on the believer in the next section.

Activities

2   Explain what a religious believer means by a 'special revelation'.

3   Explain **three** examples of special revelation.

4   'To experience a special revelation is better than experiencing a general revelation.' Do you agree? Give reasons for your answer, showing that you have thought about more than one point of view.

Discussion activity

As a whole class, discuss how the conversion of St Paul on the road to Damascus is both an example of special revelation and general revelation.

AQA   Examiner's tip

Make sure that you can explain why holy books and worship can be both general and special revelation.

Summary

You should now be able to discuss what is meant by special revelation.

The power and impact of revelation

The power of revelation

The power of revelation is to reveal God's nature to the religious believer or, in the case of Buddhism, to bring enlightenment. The power of revelation can include:

- providing proof of God's existence or belief
- helping to start off the religion
- helping people to know what they must do to live as God wishes.

Providing proof of God's existence or belief

As we have seen in the previous sections, the power of revelation is to provide people with proof that God exists. When the religious believer listens to the scriptures or performs an act of worship, the belief that what they are doing is right is reinforced.

When religious believers look at nature, its beauty and complexity convince them that this is evidence for the existence of God. The very fact that they experience the emotions of awe and wonder is further proof that nature is not the result of random chance.

The occurrence of miracles is seen by religious believers as additional evidence of God's existence. Many people saved from the sinking of the *Titanic* when it hit an iceberg were convinced that it was through some act of God that they were saved.

Discussion activity 👥👥👥

As a whole class, discuss the statement: 'Those who survived the sinking of the *Titanic* were just lucky.' Do you agree? Give reasons for your answer, showing that you have thought about more than one point of view.

Helping to start off the religion

If the founders of the different religions had not believed that the message they received was from God or, in the case of the Buddha, 'enlightenment', then the religion would not have started in the first place.

Not only did the founder have to accept the message, but then it was necessary to persuade others of the truth of what was revealed. The power of the revelation had to be sufficient for people to face persecution, and even death, rather than deny the truth of the message.

Helping people to know what they must do to live as God wishes

Having accepted that the revelations are from God, or can lead to enlightenment, the religious believer recognises that there is a specific way of life to be followed. The revelation may provide new insight into what God is like and, therefore, how the believer should respond. The revelations are a guide to how people must live as God would wish.

Objectives

Investigate the power of revelation.

Investigate the impact of revelation on those receiving it.

A *Was the fact that some people survived the sinking of the Titanic a miracle?*

🔗 links

Look back to the research that you did on the founders of religion from the research activity on page 34.

B *Sikhs accept that Guru Nanak received a revelation from God*

The impact of revelation

As we have seen, the main impact of revelation is that it is life changing. Revelations can result in people changing not only their way of life, but also their religion. For example, St Paul converted from Judaism to Christianity.

Having accepted the revelation is true, then the power of the revelation is to change the way in which people live their lives. This can affect the way they eat and drink, how they dress, how they treat others and even the laws of a country.

Commitment to their religion may influence the way in which people worship, as they seek to become closer to God or achieve greater understanding. These acts of worship may be in private or in public.

Some religious believers consider that worship alone is not enough and that the revelations are instructing them to help the less fortunate.

Others believe that they must withdraw from everyday life for a time to give their full attention to God and/or to seek the truth. Some believers even feel that the revelation is instructing them to leave their daily lives to become a monk or nun, so that they can spend much of each day seeking to get closer to God or obtain enlightenment without the distractions of daily life.

C   Buddhist monks spend much of the day in meditation

 Examiner's tip

Make sure that you can support your answers with examples from the religion(s) you have studied.

⚭ links

Look back to the conversion of St Paul on page 19 as an example of how revelation can be life changing.

Research activity ⌐

Worship

Choose **two** of the following religions. Find out how believers of each chosen religion worship, and write a brief description.

- Buddhism
- Christianity
- Hinduism
- Judaism
- Islam
- Sikhism

Activity

'Without revelation there would be no religion.' Do you agree? Give reasons for your answer, showing that you have thought about more than one point of view.

Summary

You should now be able to explain the power and impact of revelation on those receiving it.

What is learned about the attributes of God from revelation?

There is only one God

The revelations accepted by religious believers may cause them to have a different understanding of God, but they agree that there is only one God who is the creator, controller and maintainer of the universe. The **supremacy** of God is accepted, which means that God has power over all things and is almighty. Except for Buddhism, which does not accept the existence of God, the religions studied in this book accept the idea of just one God. Some may believe that God has many forms.

Christian beliefs

Christians believe that there are three different aspects to God (the Trinity): God the Father; God the Son; and God the Holy Spirit. God the Father is the Creator, the eternal, almighty God; God the Son came to earth in the form of Jesus; and God the Holy Spirit is God as he works in the world. Christians believe that God has revealed himself to them through the Old and New Testaments (the Bible) and through the life and work of Jesus.

Hindu beliefs

Hindus believe in the one unchanging and eternal God (Brahman) who is everywhere and in everything, including each human's soul (atman). Everything comes from Brahman, who is timeless, formless and beyond human understanding. Hindus worship Brahman through many gods and goddesses that show the different aspects of God's nature. The three major aspects of Brahman are found in the three gods (the Trimurti): Brahma (the Creator); Vishnu (the Sustainer); and Shiva (the Destroyer). Hindus believe that aspects of Brahman have been revealed through their sacred writings such as the Vedas.

Jewish beliefs

Jews believe that they have a special relationship with Almighty God because God made an agreement (covenant) with them through Abraham and Moses. God will protect the Jews so long as they obey God's laws revealed through the Torah. God has revealed himself through the revelations found in the Tenakh (the Jewish sacred writings). The Tenakh are the same books as found in what Christians call the Old Testament. Jews believe that God is eternal and unlimited.

Muslim beliefs

Muslims believe in the one God, Allah, who is eternal and unchanging. Allah has no equals and is beyond human understanding. To provide some limited understanding of Allah's attributes, Muslims believe that Allah has revealed 99 of his beautiful names in the Qur'an. Attributes include Allah as All-Merciful (Ar-Rahim); the Sustainer (Ar-Razzaq); and the Greatest (Al-Kabir). Allah's final and complete revelation was sent to the Prophet Muhammad. This direct word of Allah has been recorded in the Qur'an.

Objectives

Investigate what can be learnt about the attributes of God from revelation; qualities of God such as supremacy, omnipotence, omniscience and benevolence.

Key terms

Supremacy: supreme power or authority (a quality of God).

Omnipotence: almighty, unlimited power (a quality of God).

Omniscience: the quality of knowing everything (as applied to God).

Benevolence: goodness, being all-loving (a quality of God).

Activity

1 Divide the class into three groups. Each group is to research **one** of the gods: Brahma; Vishnu; or Shiva. Each group is to report their findings about the god back to the rest of the class using presentation software.

AQA Examiner's tip

- Remember, Buddhists do not believe in God and are not theists.

Sikh beliefs

Sikhs believe that God is beyond human understanding and has numerous virtues. God is eternal and does not need anyone or anything to survive; God is self-existent. Sikhs have many names for God that they use during worship. These include Ik Onkar (the One Creator), Bhagavn (Lord or Supreme Being) and Waheguru (wonderful teacher). Sikhs believe that the one God has been revealed through the ten Gurus. The teachings of the Gurus and some writings from Islam and Hinduism have been written down in the Guru Granth Sahib.

> ### Beliefs and teachings
>
> #### The 99 Beautiful Names of Allah
>
> The most beautiful names belong to Allah: so call on him by them; but shun such men as do distort His names: for what they do, they will soon be requited.
>
> *Qur'an* 7:180

> ### Beliefs and teachings
>
> #### God is all-good
>
> 'Why do you ask me about what is good?' Jesus replied. 'There is only One who is good. If you want to enter life, obey the commandments.'
>
> *Matthew* 19:17

> ### Discussion activity
>
> With a partner, in a group or as a whole class, discuss the statement: 'There is only one God and it is wrong to think of God in different forms.' Do you agree? Give reasons for your answer, showing that you have thought about more than one point of view.

Omnipotent, omniscient and benevolent

God is believed to be **omnipotent** (all-powerful), **omniscient** (all-knowing) and **benevolent** (all-good or all-loving).

God is omnipotent

God is capable of doing anything as shown by the creation of the universe. As there are no limits to God's power, God is described as all-powerful (omnipotent).

God is omniscient

God knows all that it is possible to know – past, present and future – and is described as all-knowing (omniscient).

God is benevolent

Although God is beyond human understanding, the fact that God has created a world in which there is everything humans need for survival shows that God is all-good or all-loving (benevolent).

> ### Activities
>
> 3   Explain what is meant by the 'supremacy of God'.
> 4   What do the terms 'omnipotent' and 'omniscient' mean?
> 5   Explain what believers can learn about what God is like from holy books.

⬤⬤ links

The existence of evil and suffering has led people to question whether or not God is omnipotent, omniscient and benevolent. Find out more about the problems raised for theists by evil and suffering by reading pages 52 and 66 in Chapter 3.

> ### Research activity
>
> #### Holy books
>
> Choose **one** of the sacred texts of the religions you are studying and find out more about its importance to the religion.

> ### Beliefs and teachings
>
> #### God is all-knowing
>
> Behold, God is infinite, all-knowing… His is all that is in the heavens and on earth; all things devoutly obey His will. The Originator is He of the heavens and the earth: and when He wills a thing to be, He but says unto it, 'Be' – and it is.
>
> *Qur'an* 2:115–117

> ### Beliefs and teachings
>
> #### God is Almighty
>
> When Abram was ninety-nine years old, the LORD appeared to him and said, 'I am God Almighty; walk before me and be blameless.'
>
> *Genesis* 17:1

> ### Activity
>
> 2   Write a list of the attributes of God common to all the different religions studied in this book. For example, they all believe that God is the creator.

> ### Summary
>
> You should now be able to explain the attributes of God such as supremacy, omnipotence, omniscience and benevolence.

2.6   Does revelation show God as immanent or transcendent, personal or impersonal?

To describe God as both immanent and transcendent seems to be a contradictory way of describing God's nature. Most religions we are studying teach that God is incomprehensible, and that God's power is unlimited. God must be outside time and space as God is the creator of the universe. God is transcendent. God does not need us but we need God, as without God nothing would exist.

Yet, at the same time, many people believe that God is involved in the universe and life on earth. They believe that God was, and still is, involved in the history of the world, as can be seen in the events recorded in the sacred books of the religions. Many religious believers think that they can, and have, experienced God in their lives. God is therefore immanent.

Christians believe that God became immanent, in the form of Jesus, to show people how God wanted people to live according to his will. God remains immanent through the action of the Holy Spirit. It is an important part of Christianity that God is both transcendent and immanent.

Hindus believe that Brahman's immanence is seen through the many gods and goddesses that are aspects of Brahman. Jews believe that the immanence of God is shown through the Tenakh, which contains the history of God's relationship with the people of Israel. Muslims believe that Allah has communicated with the prophets throughout history until the final revelation was sent to Muhammad. God knows what each person does, and will reward or punish people after death. Sikhs believe that God is present in the universe and also within each human being.

Do the revelations show God as personal or impersonal?

Religions believe that no other being has the power of God. God the creator may be a force or power with whom it is not possible to have a **personal** relationship. To think of God as personal would mean that God would have to be thought of in 'human' terms. For many religious believers, this would be unacceptable and God remains **impersonal**. They can pray to God but must always remember that God is beyond human understanding. However, this does not mean that God is not close to them.

Most Christians believe that it is possible to have a personal relationship with God. They believe that they can talk to God through prayer and listen to his reply. Many Christians believe that God has revealed himself as the perfect 'Father' – a father who loves and cares for his children, and wants the best for them, but allows them the freedom to make mistakes and hopefully grow as a result. As a good father, God guides and disciplines his children. God will judge his 'children' on how they have lived by his rules and the relationship with God is therefore personal. For most Christians, God can be both personal and impersonal.

Objectives

Investigate what can be learned about God as immanent, transcendent, personal and impersonal from revelation.

∞ **links**

Look back to page 31 to remind yourself of the meanings of 'immanent' and 'transcendent'.

A   Christians believe that God became immanent in the form of Jesus

Key terms

Personal nature (of God): the idea that God is an individual or person with whom people are able to have a relationship or feel close to.

Impersonal nature (of God): the idea that God has no 'human' characteristics, is unknowable and mysterious, more like an idea or force.

With a partner, in a small group or as a whole class, discuss what you think Muslims mean when they describe Allah as being closer to them 'than their jugular vein'. Does this make Allah personal or impersonal?

Is God immanent or transcendent, personal or impersonal?

For some religious believers, God can be all four things at once as for God everything is possible. God is transcendent and impersonal but can still be experienced by people through, for example, prayer and worship, when the believer feels that there is a personal relationship with God. In this way, the believer is able to have a meaningful relationship with God. When God is involved in the events of the world, God is immanent.

Whatever the belief, all the religions agree that God remains beyond human understanding and a mystery. What is known of God results from God's revelations to humans.

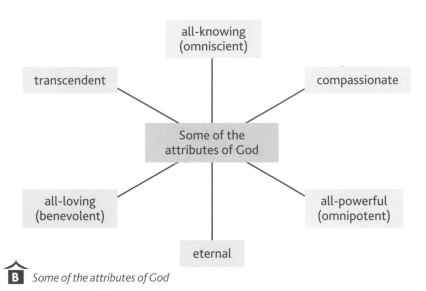

B Some of the attributes of God

You need to be able to explain, using examples, how God can be immanent and/or transcendent; personal and/or impersonal.

1 Copy the spider diagram above, showing some of the attributes of God. Learn the terms on the diagram.

2 Explain the meaning of the terms 'transcendent', 'omniscient' and 'omnipotent'.

3 Explain the difference between the belief that God is personal and the belief that God is transcendent.

4 'It is wrong to describe God as a person.' Do you agree? Give reasons for your answer, showing that you have thought about more than one point of view.

Summary

You should now be able to explain what religious believers learn from revelation about God as immanent, transcendent, personal and impersonal.

General revelation and special revelation

The strengths of general revelation

The strengths of general revelation when compared to special revelation include the following:

- General revelation is indirect and available to everyone, whereas special revelation is only for the individual or group that receives it. Everyone has access to the sacred texts through which God or enlightenment can be revealed.

- General revelation has been available to everyone at all times and in all places throughout human history, whereas special revelation is for an individual or a group at a specific time and place.

- General revelation is therefore continuous and ongoing, which means that, as new issues arise, a religion is able to update its thinking accordingly. A special revelation is specific to a time in history and may therefore be outdated for modern society.

- Conscience is available to all religious believers as a general revelation, and therefore guides them in the right and wrong way of understanding the revelations or the behaviour expected of them.

The strengths of special revelation

The strengths of special revelation when compared to general revelation include the following:

- Special revelation discloses the whole of what God wants people to know, whereas general revelation only discloses part. For example, the Prophet Muhammad is believed to have received the total revelation from Allah – the Qur'an.

- Special revelation is direct and, because it is received first-hand, it often has a stronger, more immediate impact. Individuals and groups know that it is the exact truth.

- People who experience special revelation possess an authority and confidence that enable them to lead others to faith through general revelation of their direct experience.

The importance of general and special revelations

Many religious believers would argue that both general and special revelations are needed together as proof of the existence of God. Special revelation is available to an individual or group, and requires interpretation, and this happens through general revelation.

Objectives

Examine the strengths and weaknesses of general revelation.

Examine the strengths and weaknesses of special revelation.

⊂⊃ links

Look back to page 26 to remind yourself of what is meant by faith.

Look back to pages 32–35 to remind yourself of the difference between general and special revelation.

A *A sacred text can be both general and special revelation*

Special and general revelations in Christianity

The Holy Book (i.e. sacred writings) of Christians is the Bible. When Christians read the Bible, it can affect them so deeply that they feel they have a special revelation of God's presence; that God is communicating with them directly. All Christians can read the accounts of special revelations in the Bible, such as miracles and visions. The fact that these accounts are available to everyone means that the Bible can be regarded as general revelation.

The Bible is not one book. It is a collection of 66 books written over many centuries. As the Bible covers a long period of time, most Christians agree that the Bible reveals:

- how God has acted in the history of the world
- how God wants people to live their lives
- what God is like.

Christians believe that it is through studying the Bible that God reveals how he wants people to live their lives and what he is like. For example, the Ten Commandments (Old Testament) and the teachings of Jesus (New Testament) are sources of moral authority.

B   *The Bible is the holy book of Christians*

I   THOU SHALT HAVE NO OTHER GODS BEFORE ME

II   THOU SHALT NOT MAKE UNTO THEE ANY GRAVEN IMAGE

III   THOU SHALT NOT TAKE THE NAME OF THE LORD THY GOD IN VAIN

IV   REMEMBER THE SABBATH DAY, TO KEEP IT HOLY

V   HONOUR THY FATHER AND THY MOTHER

VI   THOU SHALT NOT KILL

VII   THOU SHALT NOT COMMIT ADULTERY

VIII   THOU SHALT NOT STEAL

IX   THOU SHALT NOT BEAR FALSE WITNESS AGAINST THY NEIGHBOUR

X   THOU SHALT NOT COVET

C   *The Ten Commandments are a form of revelation in the Old Testament*

Discussion activity

As a whole class, discuss whether or not it is possible for religious believers to have complete faith in their religion without having a special revelation.

Activities

1   Explain how special revelation is different from general revelation.

2   'General revelation is the best way to know God.' Do you agree? Give reasons for your answer, showing that you have thought about more than one point of view.

Summary

You should now be able to evaluate the strengths and weaknesses of general revelation versus special revelation.

Revelation – reality or illusion?

▊ Is revelation real?

One of the issues that religions and religious believers have to face is proving to themselves, and to others, whether or not any revelation is genuine. Religious believers need to find evidence to support their claims that revelation is true.

The difficulty of proving the reality of any revelation

The problems for religious believers in proving the **reality** of any revelation include the following:

- Special revelations occur to specific individuals and groups. They are therefore subjective and difficult to prove. It is not possible to prove that the revelations are true through observation or scientific testing.

- General revelations are available to everyone. However, there are conflicting interpretations of them between the different religions and within the religions themselves. Therefore, it is not possible to determine which of the different claims about revelations are true.

Evidence to support the reality of any revelation

When looking for evidence that a revelation is real, religious people might ask these questions:

- Does the revelation correspond to things in the real world? For example, if the revelation says that people can fly, then people would know that it cannot be true as this is a false statement. However, if the revelation states that water in a particular place will cure people, and it does, then the revelation is proved to be true.

- Does the revelation fit in with earlier revelations accepted by the religion? If it does, it may be true. If it contradicts other revelations, then some people may argue that it is not genuine.

- Does the revelation change an atheist or agnostic to a belief in God? If it does, it may be genuine.

- Does the revelation convert someone from one religion to another (for example, the experience of Saul – later St Paul – on the road to Damascus)? If it does, it may be genuine.

▊ Is revelation an illusion?

Atheists would argue that as God does not exist, then any revelation is an **illusion**. It is not genuine. Religious believers have to find evidence to prove to themselves and others that a revelation is true.

A *We know the moon exists because we can see it for ourselves*

Key terms

Reality: the quality or state of being actual or true.

Illusion: an erroneous perception of reality.

Discussion activity 👥

With a partner, in a small group or as a whole class, discuss whether or not the reality of any revelation can ever be proved.

Why atheists consider any revelation to be an illusion

Atheists reject the reality of revelation for these reasons:

- It is a false experience brought on by alcohol or drugs. The religious believer thinks that they have had a revelation, but in fact nothing really happened.
- The believer is so desperate to have a revelation that they believe they have received one. It is wishful thinking.
- The person may be suffering from a physical or mental illness that makes them hear voices, and they mistakenly believe that they have received revelations.
- The mind can play tricks and there may be another explanation for what has happened to someone claiming to have had a revelation.
- The fact that there are conflicting revelations between different religions is evidence that they are not true.

Research activity

Mirages

Mirages could be used as evidence to show that the mind can play tricks. Using the internet and/or a library, find out how mirages are illusions.

B   *A mirage is an optical illusion caused by atmospheric conditions, especially heat*

Why religious believers accept revelation

Religious believers accept that some revelations are genuine.

- Religious believers would look to the effect on individuals and groups as evidence that a revelation is genuine. The fact that millions follow the major religions and people have been willing to die because of their faith, make it likely that the revelations are genuine.
- If there is no reason to doubt the word of the person, then why reject what they have to say? If the person does not lie, then why should they falsely claim that they have had a revelation?
- There is a common core of beliefs found in any revelation that would support the revelation as true because it matches scientific observations.

Activity

'It is wrong to reject any revelation as an illusion.' Do you agree? Give reasons for your answer, showing that you have thought about more than one point of view.

AQA   Examiner's tip

Make sure that you know what is meant by the terms 'reality' and 'illusion'.

Summary

You should now be able to discuss the issues of reality and illusion in terms of any revelation.

Alternative explanations for claims of revelation

▮ What are the alternatives?

The previous section considered reasons why atheists reject the claims of religious believers that revelations are genuine. This section considers alternative explanations for claims of revelation.

Revelation as the result of a type of epilepsy

Scientists researching into religious experience, such as Dr Michael Persinger, believe that some revelations are the result of the individual experiencing temporal lobe epilepsy (a type of epilepsy that affects the part of the brain involved in speech, memory and hearing). While having an epileptic fit, the person believes that he or she has had a vision in which they received a revelation.

One of these people, whose revelations are claimed by scientists to be the result of temporal lobe epilepsy, is Ellen White. The claim is that her revelations occurred only after she had a head injury and began to have epileptic fits. Believers in Ellen White's spirituality (the sense of something that is outside normal human experience) would deny this to be the case, claiming that there is no evidence that she made up the revelations, or ever had seizures or mental illness. Often the revelations were received when others were present and no one reported that she had fits.

Objectives

Investigate alternative explanations for claims of revelation.

Activity

1 Look back to pages 44–45 and list the reasons atheists would give for rejecting revelations as genuine.

Case study

Ellen G. White

Ellen G. White (1827–1915) was a Christian whose revelations led to the founding of the Church of the Seventh Day Adventists. Through her visions, she revealed to her followers how they should live and worship. She described her visions as involving a bright light that would surround her. She would find herself with Jesus or angels, who would reveal to her past and future events, and places such as heaven and other planets.

A *Ellen G. White (1827–1915)*

The Revelations of Ellen White

Now science has afforded a new spin on White's spirituality. A leading neurologist who has studied White's personal history and opus has concluded that, rather than being divinely inspired, her illusions stemmed from a form of epilepsy. 'Her whole clinical course suggested to me the high probability that she had temporal lobe epilepsy,' says Gregory Holmes, a neurologist at Dartmouth Medical School in New Hampshire. The multitude of visions, Holmes suggests, were actually epileptic seizures.

The Times, 17 April 2003

Revelations as the result of wishful thinking

The believer may be so desperate to fit in with the other members of the religion that they think that they have had a revelation. This may occur, for example, if an individual cannot become a full member of the faith until they have had a revelation of the truth of its teaching. Some Pentecostal Christian denominations teach that a sign that a person is saved is often given to the congregation by the believer demonstrating the gift of 'speaking in tongues'. An individual may be so eager to be accepted into the denomination that they make up the experience.

Ordinary events interpreted as revelations

The ways in which people interpret an experience and whether or not they believe that they have had a revelation depends on their religious beliefs. For example, an atheist and a religious believer can look at the same landscape but how they interpret what they see will be different. The atheist will continue to see a beautiful landscape, but the theist will see it as a revelation of God's existence.

Fraudulent 'revelations'

Some 'revelations' have been exposed as confidence tricks. These were later discovered to have been invented for the purpose of the individual gaining fame or money. In the 1980s, for example, Jimmy and Tammy Faye Bakker set themselves up as Christian televangelists and used spiritual guidance as a means of making money for themselves.

Conscience as a result of the way you were brought up

Religious believers argue that conscience is one of the ways in which people receive revelations. They claim the evidence for this is the fact that people know the difference between right and wrong. The psychiatrist, Sigmund Freud, denied that revelations are from God. For example, Freud argued that the reason why people have guilt feelings is because of the way they were raised and has nothing to do with God. If you were brought up to believe that eating pork is wrong, then you will feel guilty if you eat pork.

AQA   Examiner's tip

You need to be able to show that you have thought about more than one point of view when considering whether or not revelations are genuine.

⚭ links

Look back to page 24 to remind yourself of why some people think guilt feelings are not from God.

Discussion activity 👥

As a whole class, discuss the responses that you think religious believers would give to these alternative explanations for claims of revelation.

Activity

2   'Genuine revelations do not happen.' Do you agree? Give reasons for your answer, showing that you have thought about more than one point of view.

Summary

You should now be able to discuss the alternative explanations for claims of revelation.

Why believers find it difficult to accept the reality of some examples of revelation

■ Difficulties in accepting the reality of a revelation

The previous two sections described the reasons non-believers give for rejecting revelations as genuine. Atheists do not believe in the existence of God, therefore they do not accept the reality of revelations. However, religious believers also have to overcome problems in accepting the reality of revelation. These problems include:

- conflicting claims to the truth from different religions
- conflicting claims to the truth within the same religion
- different perspectives on, or interpretations of, the revelation.

Conflicting claims to the truth from different religions

Religious believers have to consider the problem that if revelations reveal the reality of how things are, then why are there conflicting claims to the truth from the different religions? Buddhists do not believe in God, and within the other faiths there are different understandings of God. For example, Hindus and Christians believe that God is revealed in different forms but Muslims, Jews and Sikhs reject such an idea. There may also be differences in the way in which religions believe that God wishes people to live. The Qur'an forbids the drinking of alcohol, but in the New Testament Jesus changes water into wine.

Conflicting claims to the truth within the same religion

Even within the same religion, there are different interpretations of the meaning of particular revelations. For example, in Islam, Muslims do not agree as to whether or not the revelation in the Qur'an demands that women are to cover their face in public.

An example of conflicting claims to the truth within the same religion can also be found in Christianity. Christians agree that God inspired the Bible and that it is one way in which God has made himself known to the world. However, Christians do not agree how God has 'spoken' through the Bible and how particular Bible passages are to be interpreted. This is why, for some Christians, the Bible is a special revelation and for others it is a general revelation.

Research activity

Different Christian interpretations of the Bible

Using the internet and/or a library, research the differences of interpretation of the Bible between Fundamentalists who believe the Bible is the literal Word of God and other Christians who believe that the Bible is the Word of God interpreted by human beings.

Different perspectives on revelation

Worship may be classed as both special and general revelation, according to whether it is believed that God has made himself known directly or indirectly to the believer. For example, when religious

Objectives

Examine the problems for believers in accepting the reality of a revelation.

Consider responses of believers to the problems.

⚭ links

Look back to pages 44–47 to see the reasons given for rejecting revelations as genuine and some of the responses given by religious believers.

Activities

1 Read the account of the miracle at Cana in the New Testament, John 2:1–11.

2 Write an account of the miracle at Cana.

⚭ links

Look back to pages 38–39 for the different beliefs about God.

Extension activities

1 Using the internet and/ or a library, find out how Sunni Muslims interpret the Qur'an in different ways from Shi'ite Muslims.

2 Write an explanation of the conflicting claims to the truth between Sunnis and Shi'ites.

A *If every revelation is genuine, why are there so many different ways of worship?*

believers claim to feel the direct presence of God during an act of worship, this is special revelation. For other believers, the desire to worship God is general revelation. If God exists, then why does God not reveal himself to everyone directly?

How do religious believers respond to these difficulties?

Many religious believers have faith that their revelation is the right one. Therefore, where there is conflict between different revelations, they argue that it is the other believers who have misinterpreted their revelations. Islam, for example, points out that the sacred writings of other religions have been translated from the original language, or collected together over a long period of time, and this has resulted in errors. The Qur'an, however, was written down as Muhammad received the revelations and has remained in the original language; it has, therefore, not been changed by human intervention. Some believers are prepared to allow that there may be different ways of becoming close to God, and that their faith is just one of those.

links

The term 'worship' is covered in more detail on pages 18–19 in Chapter 1, or you can look it up in the Glossary at the back of this book.

AQA Examiner's tip

You need to be able to show that you have thought about more than one point of view when considering the difficulties associated with revelations.

Activities

3 Explain **three** problems for believers in accepting the reality of a revelation.

4 'The revelations of the different religions cannot be genuine because they do not agree with each other.' Do you agree? Give reasons for your answer, showing that you have thought about more than one point of view.

Summary

You should now be able to explain the difficulties for believers in accepting the reality of a revelation and how they respond to these difficulties.

2

Remember to read the question carefully and select the important points when you are writing an answer to an examination question.

Revelation – summary

For the examination you should be able to explain:

✔ what is meant by revelation and ideas of God's self-revelation to humanity

✔ what is meant by 'general' and 'special' revelations

✔ the differences between general and special revelations

✔ the power of any type of revelation, and its impact on those receiving the revelation

✔ what is learned about God from the revelation.

You should also be able to evaluate:

✔ the comparative strengths and weaknesses of general and special revelations

✔ the issues of reality or illusion when considering any revelation

✔ alternative explanations for claims of revelation

✔ the problems for believers in accepting the reality of a revelation.

Sample answer

1 Write an answer to the following examination question:

'God can only be known through revelation.' Do you agree? Give reasons for your answer, showing that you have thought about more than one point of view. Refer to religious arguments in your answer. *(6 marks)*

2 Read the following sample answer:

> I agree that God can be known through revelation because I believe that my holy book is the way God has spoken to us. I think God sent this revelation so that people can learn something about God. I do not think it is the only way that God is revealed, as I think that when we look at nature we can feel the presence of God in his creation. Also, when I pray I feel that God is listening to me and that sometimes he answers my prayers.

3 With a partner, discuss the sample answer. Do you think that there are other things that the student could have included in the answer?

4 What mark would you give this answer out of 6? (Look at the mark scheme in the Introduction on page 7 (AO2) before you attempt this.) What are the reasons for the mark you have given?

AQA Examination-style questions

1 Look at the photograph and answer the following questions.

(a) Give **two** examples of special revelation. *(2 marks)*

(b) Explain briefly how general revelation is different from special revelation. *(3 marks)*

(c) 'Revelations are illusions.' What do you think? Explain your opinion. *(3 marks)*

(d) Explain, using an example, how a religious conversion is an example of special revelation. *(4 marks)*

(e) 'Revelations prove that God exists.' Do you agree? Give reasons for your answer, showing that you have thought about more than one point of view. Refer to religious arguments in your answer. *(6 marks)*

Examiner's tip Remember that when you are given a statement and asked 'do you agree?' you must show what you think and the reasons why other people might take a different view. If your answer is one-sided, you can only achieve a maximum of 4 marks. If you make no comment about religious belief or practice, you will achieve no more than 3 marks.

3.1   The problem of suffering

■ An imperfect world

On Boxing Day 2004, many people woke to news that an undersea earthquake in the Indian Ocean had triggered giant waves that wiped out huge areas of coastline in Indonesia, Sri Lanka, Thailand and India. Over the next few days, it became clear that the 'tsunami' had killed over 225,000 people in 11 countries. One-third of the dead were children. A father described how he clung to a tree and could do nothing to stop his wife, seven-year-old son and two-month-old twins being swept away. The suffering did not end there. Survivors had also lost their homes and jobs. The sea water created serious long-lasting damage to ecosystems, freshwater supplies and the soil.

A *People lost families, homes and jobs in the 2004 tsunami*

Where is God when people suffer? Is this God's judgement? If God exists, what kind of God would allow children to be killed? What about the animals and plant life? Did God know this would happen? Is there any meaning in all of this **suffering**?

■ Why suffering is a problem

Most of us have not experienced a major natural disaster. We may have floods, storms and even earthquakes but loss of life is usually rare. Yet, we all suffer pain, illness, loss and, finally, death. So suffering is a problem for all of us.

Suffering raises problems for theists, who believe that God is benevolent (all-good and all-loving), omniscient (all-knowing) and omnipotent (all-powerful).

Key terms

Suffering: when people have to face and live with unpleasant events or conditions.

Responsibility: duty; the idea that we are in charge of our own actions.

BURMA DEATH TOLL WORSE THAN TSUNAMI

CHINA EARTHQUAKE KILLS THOUSANDS

B *Did these people deserve what happened to them?*

∞ links

Look back to page 9 to remind yourself of the meaning of theist.

■ Questions for believers

■ If God is all-good and wants the best for people, why does God allow suffering that is clearly not good? Are God's intentions bad? What is his purpose?

■ If God is benevolent, why does God allow us to suffer? Surely, if he cares for us and wants us to be happy, he would not want us to suffer pain and loss. (If God wills our suffering, he is cruel.)

■ If God is omniscient, he must realise that we suffer. Knowledge brings **responsibility** with it. How can he stand by and do nothing to stop our suffering?

■ If God is omnipotent and can do anything, God could prevent suffering or stop it altogether. Yet suffering continues. Theists believe that God created the world. If that is so, why did he create a world that contains so much death and destruction? (If God cannot stop our suffering, then he is not all-powerful.)

■ Why does God allow innocent people to suffer? What purpose does it serve? People who have lived good and decent lives, children who have not done anything wrong, why should these innocent people suffer?

○○ links

Look back to pages 38–39 to remind yourself of the meaning of benevolent, omniscient and omnipotent.

Activities

Answer the following questions, giving reasons for your answers.

1 Can anyone live a pain-free life?

2 What would the world be like if no one suffered or died?

3 Do some people deserve to suffer?

Discussion activities

With a partner, in a group or as a whole class, discuss the following statements:

1 'God cannot be loving and let people suffer.'

2 'Suffering and pain are never the will of God.'

Give reasons for your answers, showing that you have thought about more than one point of view.

AQA   *Examiner's tip*

You need to be able to give reasons why suffering is a problem for theists, and outline the questions suffering raises about God's love, power and purpose.

Extension activity

Collect news articles or personal accounts of how people suffer in today's world. Make a note of who, or what, caused the suffering in each case.

Summary

You should now understand that theists believe in an all-good, all-loving, all-knowing and all-powerful God, and be able to explain how suffering raises questions about why such a God allows suffering to exist in the world that he created.

Reasons for suffering

Who is to blame?

Suffering falls into two main categories:

1 **Natural suffering** caused by natural events such as earthquakes, volcanoes, floods, hurricanes or drought.

2 **Man-made suffering** caused as a result of people acting in a way that hurts themselves or other people. Sometimes this form of suffering is an accident, for example a driver who hits a child running out from between parked cars. Sometimes it is deliberate, for example, murder, theft, rape or abuse.

Some suffering is *both* natural and caused by human actions. The cyclone that caused so much destruction in Burma could not have been prevented, but the delay in getting help to the people who were affected cost many more lives and could have been avoided. People must take some of the responsibility for the suffering of others.

Natural suffering

Most natural suffering is no one's fault; it is just the way the earth has developed over millions of years. Scientists can explain the causes of earthquakes or cyclones and can sometimes even predict when they might take place, but there is not much they can do to prevent them altogether. People can build earthquake-proof buildings or flood defences to try to protect themselves from danger, but the forces of nature are powerful and beyond much of our control.

Some people would argue that God is to blame for natural suffering. If God really did create the earth, why did he create a planet where natural disasters happen? If God is powerful, why did he not make a perfect world with just the right climate and no hurricanes or earthquakes to destroy our homes?

A believer might reply to these criticisms by saying that, although God is powerful and created the earth, he is not to blame for earthquakes or bad weather! The same forces that cause volcanoes and earthquakes are the forces that formed the earth in the beginning. People should use their scientific knowledge to develop ways to avoid the suffering that these natural events cause.

Suffering caused by people

There is no simple reason for this type of suffering. People may cause suffering to others accidentally by being lazy, thoughtless or ignorant. Others may cause deliberate suffering because of hatred, greed, jealousy or selfishness. People have **free will** – they can choose how to behave. Sometimes they choose to act in a way that hurts themselves or others.

Some people might argue: if God created humans, why did he give them free will? Why did he not make them perfect so that they would always choose to do good instead of evil? If God is so good, why does he not stop people from making bad choices that hurt others?

A *A cyclone is beyond our control*

A believer might reply to these criticisms by saying that human freedom is part of our nature, just as earthquakes are part of the earth. People can think logically, can make decisions about what is right and wrong, and can feel responsibility for others. Humans are not programmed like robots always to do good; they are free to make up their own minds – therefore they may make mistakes.

B *Who is to blame?*

AQA Examiner's tip

You need to be able to explain the difference between natural and man-made suffering, and to give examples of each. You need to be able to explain how believers try to answer the questions raised about God's responsibility for suffering in the world.

Activities

2   Research the causes of **two** kinds of natural suffering.

3   Give **two** examples of suffering caused by people.

4   Consider whether it is possible for the world to be perfect.

5   Do you think that God should stop people from doing wrong? Make a list of the arguments for and against.

6   How might an atheist explain the reasons for suffering?

Discussion activities

With a partner, in a group or as a whole class, discuss the statements:

1   'God is to blame for natural suffering.'

2   'Humans are not really free if God knows what we are going to do before we do it.'

Give reasons for your answers, showing that you have thought about more than one point of view.

Summary

You should now be able to explain the difference between natural suffering and suffering caused by people, and discuss why religious people and atheists have different explanations for the reasons for suffering.

Is suffering unjust? Does it have a purpose?

Unjust suffering

It is difficult to see how the suffering of innocent children can ever have a purpose. We sometimes think that people deserve to suffer for their crimes – that their punishment is **just** – but a baby is too young to have done anything wrong. Even people who have lived good lives sometimes suffer terribly. What is the point of such cruelty? It simply seems **unjust**.

Objectives

Consider in what ways suffering is unjust.

Consider whether or not suffering has a purpose.

Key terms

Just: fair or right.
Unjust: unfair or not right.

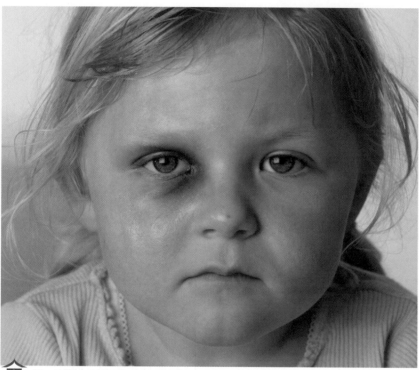

A *The suffering of an innocent child seems unjust*

Does suffering have a purpose?

Some people argue that suffering is not always bad. It sometimes has positive benefits. This may be its purpose.

- Some suffering is necessary to keep us alive and well. Pain tells us that something is wrong, so that we can do something about it. If a tooth aches, we can have it pulled out before we develop a serious infection. Pain makes us stop doing things that would cause us serious harm.

- Suffering can make us appreciate things that we take for granted. Temporary blindness, for example, can make someone appreciate the value of sight.

B *Some people risk their lives to save others*

- It can make us a better or stronger person if we have to show courage and determination to get through the difficult times. People who experience war sometimes say that it brings out the best in people – their neighbourliness, kindness and unity with others. The self-sacrifice shown by soldiers who give their lives for their country or to save their companions is an example of suffering that helps others.

- Some people suffer to achieve a goal. For example, polar explorers are willing to suffer physical hardship and put their lives at risk in order to reach the North Pole. A mother suffers pain in childbirth to bring a new life into the world.

- Some religious believers argue that suffering is a test of someone's faith. It can help people to remember their religion and God. It is easy to believe in God when everything is going well, but suffering challenges people's beliefs when life is difficult.

- Some religious people think that suffering is a punishment for sin and that it can teach us a lesson. It helps us to see what we have been doing wrong, so that we can change for the better. It is God's way of bringing people back to him.

- Another argument is that suffering is part of God's mysterious plan. We cannot explain it or see its true purpose right now because only God knows what that purpose is.

C *A mountaineer suffers to achieve a goal*

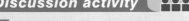

Discussion activity

1 With a partner, in a group or as a whole class, discuss the following statements:

  a 'Suffering is a punishment for doing wrong'.

  b 'The suffering of an innocent child cannot be justified.'

Give reasons for your answers, showing that you have thought about more than one point of view.

Activity

1 Answer the following questions, giving reasons for your answers.

  a Is suffering ever fair? Do some people deserve to suffer?

  b What can people learn from suffering?

  c How might a believer defend God against a charge of cruelty?

AQA Examiner's tip

You need to be able to explain how believers answer the charge that suffering is cruel and serves no purpose.

Summary

You should now be able to explain why unjust suffering is difficult for a believer to explain when defending God against a charge of cruelty, and how they try to resolve the problem.

Religious explanations for suffering

Different perspectives

Christians, Jews and Muslims believe that God gave people free will. God does not force people to make the right decisions, so people make mistakes. Suffering is a result of people choosing to do things that hurt themselves or other people.

Buddhists, Hindus and Sikhs explain suffering through the law of karma or kamma. People's thoughts and actions have consequences, here and now, or in a future life. Suffering now may be a result of bad actions in a previous life. Selfishness and sin cause suffering and should be overcome.

Buddhism

Understanding how to overcome suffering is central to Buddhism. The Four Noble Truths explain that life is unsatisfactory, full of suffering caused by craving or desire. People are selfish and never satisfied. Once one desire is fulfilled, another one arises. The three 'poisons' of ignorance, greed and hatred lead to more suffering. The way to stop suffering is to overcome desire by following the Eightfold Path.

Christianity

For Christians, suffering is a result of human freedom to choose actions that cause suffering. The story of Adam and Eve (Genesis 3) shows the consequences of free will. By disobeying God, Adam and Eve brought suffering and evil into God's perfect world. Some Christians think that suffering is a punishment for sin. It teaches a lesson so that people can grow spiritually. Some think that the devil, who tempted Adam and Eve, still tempts people to do wrong today.

Christians believe that Jesus broke the power of evil and suffering over people by his innocent suffering and death on the cross. By rising from the dead and returning to his Father in heaven, Jesus gave Christians hope that death is not the end, but that people will continue to have a relationship with God after death.

Hinduism

Hinduism teaches that suffering is a result of sinful actions in this life and past actions in previous lives. This is the law of cause and effect (karma). It is important to build up good karma, as it will help reduce suffering in the future and help people to gain release from the cycle of birth, death and rebirth.

Islam

According to the Qur'an, Allah gave Adam the world to look after but also gave him free will. This means that humans can choose to sin. Shaytan (the source of evil) was given the job of testing people's faith and character through suffering. It is believed that he does not test people more than they can bear.

Objectives

Investigate religious explanations for suffering.

links

Look back to page 54 to remind yourself of the meaning of free will.

A *There is much suffering in the world*

AQA *Examiner's tip*

You need to be able to give at least **one** religion's explanation for suffering.

Judaism

Judaism teaches that suffering results from free will given to humans. Adam and Eve brought suffering into the world by choosing to eat the forbidden fruit (Genesis 3). Jews believe that God uses suffering to train or discipline his people (Deuteronomy 8:5) and to bring people back to him (Isaiah 53:5).

The book of Job examines the problem of undeserved suffering (see Case Study below).

Sikhism

Sikhism teaches that selfish behaviour causes suffering. Suffering is a result of karma. People reap what they sow. Actions performed now affect rebirth, so it is important to do good. Why some people suffer more than others is a mystery, but Sikhs do not think that God put suffering in the world to get people to turn to him.

Beliefs and teachings

Know then in your heart that as a man disciplines his son, so the LORD your God disciplines you.

Deuteronomy 8:5

But he was pierced for our transgressions,
    he was crushed for our iniquities;
    the punishment that brought us peace was upon him,
    and by his wounds we are healed.

Isaiah 53:3

Job

Case study

In the Book of Job, Satan challenges God by claiming that if Job is sent great suffering, he will curse God and lose his faith. God allows Satan to send Job great trials – the death of his children and the loss of all his possessions. When Job still praises God, Satan sends him terrible boils that make him scrape his skin with broken pottery. Job still does not sin by cursing God. Job's friends think that his suffering is a punishment from God for sins, but Job insists that he has done nothing to deserve his ordeal and questions God. But one friend argues that God's sovereignty must not be questioned. Suffering is part of God's plan, beyond human understanding. Job repents and is rewarded with more children, a long life and twice the wealth he had before.

B   *Satan gives Job boils*

Activities

1   Explain what the story of Job teaches about suffering.
2   To what extent do religious explanations for suffering solve the problem of suffering?

Discussion activity

With a partner, in a group or as a whole class, discuss the following statement: 'A God who makes us suffer to get us to believe in him is not all-good.' Do you agree? Give reasons for your answer, showing that you have thought about more than one point of view.

AQA   Examiner's tip

'Explain' means that you need to interpret or give reasons for something. This tests your understanding. Question 1 asks you to retell the key points of the story of Job showing what the story teaches about suffering.

Summary

You should now be able to explain that Christians, Jews and Muslims believe that suffering is a result of free will, while Buddhists, Hindus and Sikhs believe suffering is a result of bad karma/kamma in this, or a previous, life.

A   *Faith-based organisations help alleviate poverty*

Practical responses

We have seen how religious people try to make sense of suffering, and how those who believe in an all-powerful, all-loving God try to answer the questions that suffering raises about their beliefs. Religions also teach their followers how to live in such a way that suffering is reduced, either for themselves or for other people. If people live good lives and follow religious teaching, they will probably not cause much suffering to others. But most religions go further than this. They teach their followers to help others who are suffering, in active practical ways. All the major religions have organisations that care for people with a wide variety of needs: the sick; the poor; asylum seekers; children with disabilities; people who have suffered bereavement and loss; and so on.

Buddhism

The Buddha taught that the way to stop suffering is to stop craving. The way to do this is by following the Eightfold Path to develop right understanding, right speech and right action. A person needs to overcome their attachment to material things or else they will always want more. Buddhists try to develop compassion for others who suffer. They practise generosity. Giving to others shows that a person is not selfish and attached to their wealth. Buddhists believe in the Middle Way, a balance between wealth and poverty. They realise that people need a certain level of economic prosperity in order to live, but that greed and hoarding money does not allow people to grow spiritually.

Christianity

Trusting in God helps Christians to accept and endure personal suffering as part of God's mysterious will, but they will try to help others who are suffering. The teaching 'Love your neighbour as yourself' (Matthew 22:39) means that Christians should not only feel compassion for those who suffer, but also should take active steps to help them. Christians should follow the example of Jesus who helped the needy and healed those who were sick.

Hinduism

To achieve release from the cycle of death and rebirth, a Hindu tries to practise yoga to develop loving devotion, self-control, knowledge and understanding through study and discipline. Hindus have a tradition of helping their families, local communities and holy men. It is their duty to give and to share with those in need.

Islam

People who cause others to suffer will be judged on the Day of Judgement. Muslims should show compassion towards people who suffer. (One of Allah's 99 names is 'The Compassionate'.) Zakah, one of the Five Pillars of Islam, requires Muslims to give a percentage of their wealth to help those in need, so relieving the suffering of the poor is an important part of Muslim belief.

Judaism

Jews are encouraged to help people who are suffering. The prophet Amos warned people not to become selfish and greedy, but to leave part of the harvest for the poor. Charity is a duty from God. It must be given sensitively so that the needy retain their self-respect and, where possible, encourage the poor to help themselves.

Sikhism

Sikhs try to rise above or transcend suffering. Selfless service (sewa) should be practised to help anyone in need. They emphasise the equality of all people and believe that sharing is an important duty, particularly with those who have little. The communal kitchen (langar) in the gurdwara (temple) serves two meals a day to every visitor, rich or poor. A free vegetarian meal is shared after every weekly service.

Activities

1 Give **three** ways in which religious people could help others who suffer.

2 Does your school support any organisations that help others? How do you help?

3 What is compassion?

Discussion activity

With a partner, in a group or as a whole class, discuss the following statement: 'Religious people can cope with suffering better than others.' Do you agree? Give reasons for your answer, showing that you have thought about more than one point of view.

Research activity

Practical responses to suffering

Using the internet and/or a library, research the work of a religious organisation that helps people who suffer.

Buddhism – www.karuna.org
Christianity – www.christianaid.org.uk
Hinduism – www.hinduaid.org
Islam – www.muslimaid.org
Judaism – www.tzedek.org.uk
Sikhism – www.khalsaaid.org

Summary

You should now be able to discuss how religions not only try to make sense of suffering, but also help those who suffer, and teach their followers to live in a way that avoids causing suffering to others.

3.6 Evil

What is meant by evil?

We often hear people use the word 'evil' to describe a horrible event or terrible crime, something that has caused great harm. It is sometimes used to describe an individual, like Hitler or Pol Pot, who has ordered the deaths of millions of people.

In the news...

The newspapers are full of stories about the suffering caused by evil actions. Here are a few examples from the *Guardian*.

China accused America of having '**evil** motives' and trying to undermine the Olympics by officially criticising China's record on human rights. (31 July 2008)

When a young couple were shot on their honeymoon in Antigua, the country's leaders urged people to remove the '**evil**' that is creeping into their society. (30 July 2008)

After 16-year-old Jimmy Mizen was murdered in an unprovoked attack in a bakery in London, his mother, despite her grief, said she felt sorry for the parents of her son's killer. 'They haven't got wonderful memories for their son,' she said, 'all they can think about is the **evil** he's done.' (12 May 2008)

A young Polish student was brutally killed and buried under the floor of a church in Glasgow. The killer... had previously spent 14 years in prison for raping two teenage girls. The judge sentenced the killer to life imprisonment for the 'inhuman' and '**evil**' attack. (5 May 2007)

Objectives

Investigate what is meant by evil.

AQA Examiner's tip

Although the problems of evil and suffering are closely linked, if you are asked about evil, be clear that you are discussing evil itself and not just suffering caused by evil actions.

Activities

1 Which of these newspaper reports do you think best describes 'evil'?
2 What do you think caused the evil that is described in these reports?

Evil actions or evil people?

Is there really a 'thing' called evil? Are there really evil people or are there just evil actions? Most of us are a mixture of good and bad. Even murderers serving life sentences may be kind to others. Many massacres and genocides have been ordered by people who genuinely believed they were serving the best interests of their country. How does someone become evil? When babies are born, they are innocent. How does an innocent child grow up into an 'evil' adult?

An evil act suggests a deliberate cruelty done in the full knowledge that it is wrong. Is there an evil force outside of people that causes bad things to happen? Or is there a supernatural **personal being**, a 'devil', which tempts people to do bad instead of good? Is evil a **psychological phenomenon**, something in people's minds that causes them to harm others or destroy life?

Key terms

Evil: the opposite of good. A force or the personification of a negative power that is seen in many traditions as destructive and against God.

Personal being (nature of evil): the idea that evil is an evil spirit or devil rather than an impersonal force.

Psychological phenomenon: an idea about the nature of evil that it is something arising from the mind of a person.

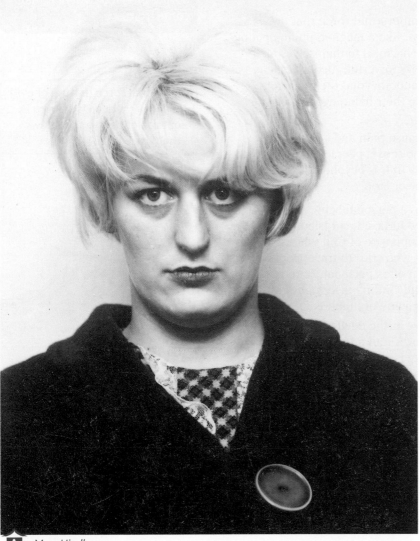

A   *Myra Hindley*

Discussion activity

With a partner, in a group or as a whole class, discuss the following statement: 'Some people are born evil.' Do you agree? Give reasons for your answer, showing that you have thought about more than one point of view.

Research activity

The Moors Murders

Using the internet and/or a library, find out about the murders committed by Ian Brady and Myra Hindley. They were described as 'evil' people. Can you find any reasons for what they did?

Myra Hindley repented of her crimes in prison and became a practising Catholic. Can people change from being evil to being good? http://news.bbc.co.uk gives a summary of the case in Myra Hindley's obituary.

Summary

You should now understand that evil is something that causes great harm to others, and be able to explain how its existence raises questions about whether people are evil in themselves or whether there are only evil actions.

Explanations for the nature of evil

There are three main explanations offered for the nature of evil. They were hinted at on page 63.

1 Some people think that evil is an **impersonal force** that draws people into doing wrong. It is almost like a magnet, pulling people towards actions that they know are harmful to themselves or to others. Sometimes evil seems very powerful. Alcoholics may describe their addiction as a force quite beyond their control; something that pulls them back into their habit, even when they know they should resist.

When terrible things happen that cause pain and suffering at random and which seem to make no sense, people often feel that there is an impersonal force at work that is beyond reason and the ability of human beings to influence or stop.

2 Other people would describe evil as a personal being or devil who causes people to sin. In Christianity, Judaism and Islam, Satan or Iblis is the source of all evil, the opposite of God who is all-good. The devil is seen as someone who tries to trick people into doing wrong. Just as God is thought of as personal, so too God's 'adversary' (the meaning of the word 'Satan') is thought to be a personal supernatural being – the enemy of humankind.

Most people today no longer believe in the devil as pictured in medieval paintings with horns, hooves and a tail, surrounded by fire, but many still believe that there is a personal being who can represent the struggle between good and evil in life.

3 Another explanation for evil comes from the study of human behaviour. Today, most people would say that evil is a psychological phenomenon, influenced by a person's upbringing or society in general, or perhaps the result of a damaged mind. Family circumstances vary, but the way parents bring up their children has a major influence on their behaviour. Young people can also be influenced by their friends and act under peer pressure, even when they know it is wrong. Society itself influences the way people act. The emphasis in the media on being rich, famous and beautiful can cause people to act in certain ways that are not always good for themselves or others.

In some cases, when horrible crimes are committed, we look for reasons in the person's background that explain, but do not excuse, their behaviour. Sometimes we think that a person who could murder a child could not possibly be sane. In some cases, this is true. They may be suffering from a mental illness or are mentally unstable and this causes them to act in a certain way.

Objectives

Investigate ideas about the nature of evil or where it may come from.

Key terms

Impersonal force (nature of evil): the idea that evil is a power outside of people that draws them to evil.

links

Look back to page 63 to remind yourself of the meaning of personal being and psychological phenomenon.

■ Who is to blame?

Some people blame God; others blame human nature.

- Evil is God's fault. He created people and gave them free will, allowing them to choose to do bad rather than good. Therefore, it is God's fault that there is evil in the world.

- Evil is our fault, not God's. Selfishness, greed and a lack of respect are simply alternatives to selflessness, generosity and respect. When we give into the 'dark' side of our nature, we do evil. God does not force us, we make the choice ourselves. There is such a thing as man-made evil.

A *The struggle between right and wrong*

Activity

1 Answer the following questions, giving reasons for your answers.

  a Do you think there is such a being as the devil?

  b What influences the way you behave?

  c Re-read the three explanations for evil. Sketch an image for each. Which do you think is the most convincing explanation?

Discussion activity

1 With a partner, in a group or as a whole class, discuss the following statements:

  a 'Blaming a person's upbringing for their evil actions is just an excuse.'

  b 'Evil is all God's fault.'

  c 'Humans are not really free if God knows what we are going to do before we do it.'

Give reasons for your answers, showing that you have thought about more than one point of view.

AQA Examiner's tip

You need to be able to explain the **three** different ideas about the nature of evil.

Summary

You should now understand three ideas about the nature of evil, and be able to discuss the opposing arguments of where evil comes from.

3.8 The problem of evil

Why evil is a problem

Evil causes suffering, so it is a problem for everybody. However, like suffering, evil creates a particular problem for people who believe in God. Theists believe that God, who created the world and human beings, is all-good, all-loving, all-powerful and all-knowing. However, the existence of evil means that he cannot be all of these things. Evil raises a number of questions for believers.

Extension activity

St Thomas Aquinas (see page 11) admitted that the existence of evil was the best argument against the existence of God. Arrange a class debate on this topic. You might like to present it as a televised *Question Time* type programme. Make sure that you consider different viewpoints.

Questions for believers

- If God is all-good, why did he create a world where evil is present?
- If God is all-loving, surely he would want his creations to be good too, in the same way that a loving parent would not want their child to behave badly.
- If God is all-powerful, why can he not stop someone before they do evil? If God can do anything, he could stop a murderer from killing, or a thief from stealing. At the very least, he could prevent circumstances that might lead to these crimes. Yet evil continues, so it seems that God cannot do anything to prevent evil. This makes some people say that God is weak.
- If God is all-knowing, he must know that people will sometimes choose evil over good. Why did God give people free will to make that choice?
- Some believers say that everything that happens is the will of God. Does God want evil to happen? This seems to contradict his goodness and care for people.

A *Sometimes people struggle to reconcile belief in God with evil in the world*

Answers

- Religious people would say that the very fact that God gave people the freedom to make their own decisions about right and wrong, shows his goodness and love. He did not create robots that were programmed to do good all the time but gave humans free will, despite the risk that they would use their freedom to hurt others. God is like a loving parent who allows his children to make mistakes and learn from experience.
- Some believers would say that, although God is all-powerful and can defeat evil, he chooses not to use that power to force people to use their freedom wisely. If he interfered every time someone was about to commit an evil act, he would be controlling people and they would not be free.

- Other believers do not think that everything that happens is God's will. This would mean that people were not really free to make their own choices because everything would be fixed or determined in advance. God does not want evil to happen, but, unfortunately, people go against his will.

B   *Why does God allow evil?*

AQA   *Examiner's tip*

You need to be able to explain why evil is a problem for theists, and how religious people answer the questions it raises about the existence of a loving, powerful God.

Activities

1   Why is evil a problem for people who believe in God? Explain your opinion.

2   Are the answers given above convincing? Explain your opinion.

Discussion activity

1   With a partner, in a group or as a whole class, discuss the following statements:

a   'If God allows people freedom, he cannot be all-powerful.'

b   'If there was no evil, there would be no goodness.'

Give reasons for your answers, showing that you have thought about more than one point of view.

Summary

You should now be able to discuss how evil raises questions for believers about God's love and power, and how they base their response on human freedom of choice.

▪ Different perspectives

Christians, Jews and Muslims share the view that God/Allah gave people free will to choose evil or good. Human beings wilfully misuse God's gift of freedom, so evil is their fault, not God's.

Buddhists, Hindus and Sikhs see the source of evil as ignorance, a wrong understanding of the way things really are. The law of karma/kamma requires people to think about their own responsibility for evil, and whether their actions now, or in a previous life, contributed to its cause.

Buddhism

Buddhists believe that evil is caused by people's selfish desires or craving. The root causes of evil are the three 'poisons' of greed, hatred and ignorance. In order to overcome these three poisons, Buddhists try to practise generosity, loving kindness and right understanding or wisdom.

Christianity

Christians believe that everything God made was perfect. Evil came into the world through Adam and Eve's disobedience, sometimes called original sin. When Satan tempted them to eat from the forbidden 'tree of knowledge of good and evil', they realised that they had freedom to choose between right and wrong and would now be responsible for their own actions. When people rebel against God's laws, evil results. People need salvation (rescuing) from sin. Christians believe that Jesus was the 'second Adam' who restored people's broken relationship with God.

Hinduism

Hindus believe that evil is part of the cycle of birth, death and rebirth. Hindu scriptures tell stories of gods fighting the forces of evil in the world. The story of Rama and Sita, which Hindus remember at Divali, is one such story in which the power of good triumphs over the power of evil. God is like the sun – all light and no darkness – so God is not the source of evil. Just as people cast a shadow when they turn away from the sun, so evil is a sort of absence of God that takes hold when people turn their backs on him. The law of karma means that people can make up for evil actions in this or a previous life by living a good and dutiful life.

Islam

Muslims believe that Allah created a perfect world, including some beings called Jinn who, like humans, had free will. A Jinn called Iblis refused to bow down to Adam as Allah had commanded. Iblis (renamed Shaytan, 'the refuser') tempted Adam and Hawa (Eve) to disobey Allah. Shaytan, the source of evil, still tries to turn people away from Allah. On the Day of Judgement, evil-doers will be called to account and punished. Allah is merciful and compassionate, so those who truly repent will be forgiven. Muslims do not believe in original

Objectives

To consider religious explanations for the origins of evil.

A *Adam and Eve disobeyed God*

sin. Everyone starts life with a clean slate, but must submit to the will of Allah and resist temptation. Allah's plan for humans means nothing can happen unless he wills it. Allah gives people free will, but knows the outcome of their choices.

Judaism

Jews believe that God created everything, including evil. God is all-powerful, so evil must be under his control. In the Bible, Satan is created and controlled by God, but also fights against God. Satan represents the tendency people have to stray from the path of righteousness and faith. God is all-loving, so he must have created evil for a good purpose, to allow people freedom to have real choices. God wants people to act justly, be merciful, and walk humbly with God, but he does not force them. People can freely choose to reject God, but if everyone followed God's laws, evil would have no power.

B *People can choose to overcome these evils*

Beliefs and teachings

He has showed you, O man, what is good.
        And what does the LORD require of you?
        To act justly and to love mercy
        and to walk humbly with your God.

Micah 6:8

Sikhism

Sikhs believe that God created humankind and a spark of his divine presence is in everyone, so they should be respected. Humans are not evil by nature, but they are ignorant and self-centred. They forget to see God in others. This stops them from realising the truth and doing good. God is the source of everything, both good and evil. People are free to choose between good and evil. Sikhs talk about five evils: anger; attachment; greed; lust; and pride. It is up to each person to overcome these.

Activities

1 Explain the teaching of **one** religion about the reasons for evil.
2 Do you find the explanations for evil convincing? Give your reasons.

Discussion activity

With a partner, in a group or as a whole class, discuss the following statement: 'Evil is the absence of God.' Do you agree? Give reasons for your answer, showing that you have thought about more than one point of view.

Summary

You should now be able to discuss different religious explanations for the origins of evil.

AQA Examiner's tip

You need to be able to describe the way in which at least **one** religion explains the origins of evil in the world.

■ Ways of responding

All religions have codes of conduct or rules for living to avoid doing evil to others. But how should believers respond when evil is done to them or when great evils occur in the world or in society?

Objectives

Consider how religious believers should, and do, respond in the face of evil.

Buddhism

The Eightfold Path contains five moral precepts that forbid: harming living things (killing); stealing; lying; misusing the senses (misusing sex); and taking drugs and alcohol, which cloud the mind. Buddhists practise meditation to train the mind to avoid evil thoughts. Evil actions have evil consequences, so retaliation is avoided. Hatred is never appeased by hatred; hatred is appeased by love (Dhammapada 5).

Christianity

Jesus commanded Christians to love God and their neighbour. He taught people to love their enemies and, when evil is done to them, to 'turn the other cheek'. The Lord's Prayer says that people must forgive others so that God can forgive them.

A *Buddhist monks protesting against the Vietnam War in the 1960s*

Beliefs and teachings

Forgive us our sins,
        for we also forgive everyone who sins against us,
And lead us not into temptation.

Luke 11:4

Many Christians worked tirelessly against the great evil of racial discrimination in the USA. Martin Luther King Jr, a Christian minister, won rights for black people through peaceful, non-violent protest.

Hinduism

Hindus meditate and practise yoga to gain control of their bodies and minds, to overcome selfishness, greed and anger and to seek union with God. They respect life and do not harm living things. Most Hindus are vegetarians. Goodness to others gains good karma. When facing evil, many Hindus are inspired by Mahatma Gandhi (1869–1948), who used non-violent protest to help India gain independence from British rule.

Islam

Muslims live by the Five Pillars: faith in Allah and his prophet Muhammad; prayer; almsgiving; fasting; and pilgrimage to Makkah. Allah will judge them on Judgement Day, so Muslims try to live in complete submission to his will and in peace with others. The Qur'an teaches Muslims to stand up for justice and what is right. Muhammad Ali was stripped of his boxing title and was prepared to face jail in the USA for his belief that the Vietnam War was evil.

B *Mahatma Gandhi*

Judaism

Jews believe that God has made a covenant (agreement) with them to protect and save them if they keep his laws and live holy lives. Evil can be overcome by complete obedience to God. Evil-doers can expect punishment. Just as a father disciplines his son, so God disciplines humans.

The great evil of the Holocaust was a huge test of Jewish faith in God. Although some have lost their faith, many Jews campaign for human rights and record survivors' stories to try to prevent future atrocities.

Beliefs and teachings

Know then in your heart that as a man disciplines his son, so the LORD your God disciplines you.

Deuteronomy 8:5

Children in the Holocaust

Over 1.5 million children died in the Holocaust. The Nazis wanted to create a racially pure society. Jewish children were first expelled from German schools and banned from parks or swimming baths. Then, disabled children, considered 'useless eaters', were taken from their parents for a supposed 'cure', but were secretly killed. Many children died from starvation and disease in the ghettoes. Mothers and children were often the first to be gassed at concentration camps because they were not strong enough to be 'selected' for slave labour.

Case study

Sikhism

The Gurus taught Sikhs to practise selfless service and put God at the centre of their lives. The Rahit Maryada, a code of conduct for a virtuous life, emphasises prayer, meditation, a disciplined life, and strong family and community values. Sikhs try to practise five virtues of self-control, truth, patience, perfect faith and compassion. Guru Nanak opposed evils of his day, for example the belief that some people were 'untouchable' (so low in status that they should be avoided) and the custom of a wife throwing herself on her husband's funeral pyre (sati).

Activities

1 Explain how believers in **one** religion have responded to injustice.
2 Why might an event like the Holocaust challenge someone's faith in God?

Discussion activity

With a partner, in a group or as a whole class, discuss the following statement: 'It is impossible to respond to evil with love.' Do you agree? Give reasons for your answer, showing that you have thought about more than one point of view.

Research activity

One religion's response to a particular evil

Using the internet and/or a library, find out how religious believers from **one** religion have responded to a particular evil.

AQA   Examiner's tip

You need to be able to explain how religious people *should* respond to evil, and also how they *have responded* to evil in a particular example.

Summary

You should now be able to explain how religious people should respond to evil by trying to overcome it in their own lives and in society, and how many have responded by protesting against evil actions in society.

3

AQA *Examiner's tip*

Remember that you may refer to one or more than one religion or denomination in this part of the examination.

The problems of evil and suffering – summary

For the examination you should now be able to:

✔ explain why evil and suffering are problems for people who believe in God

✔ outline the questions that evil and suffering raise for theists

✔ explain the differences between natural and man-made suffering

✔ discuss whether or not suffering is unjust or has a purpose

✔ discuss what evil is and where it comes from

✔ outline religious explanations for evil and responses to it

✔ explain how religious believers resolve the problems of evil and suffering

✔ outline how religious believers respond to evil and suffering.

Sample answer

1 Write an answer to the following examination question:

'All suffering has a purpose.' Do you agree? Give reasons for your answer, showing that you have thought about more than one point of view. Refer to religious arguments in your answer.

(6 marks)

2 Read the following sample answer:

> I agree that suffering has a purpose. If people did not feel pain, they would not realise they were ill. Sometimes suffering makes a person stronger because they have come through a bad period in their lives with courage and determination. On the other hand, some suffering does not seem to have a purpose. Some suffering is totally pointless like the children in China who died in the earthquake.

3 With a partner, discuss the sample answer. Do you think that there are other things that the student could have included in the answer?

4 What mark would you give this answer out of 6? (Look at the mark scheme in the Introduction on page 7 (AO2) before you attempt this.) What are the reasons for the mark you have given?

AQA Examination-style questions

1 Look at the photograph and answer the following questions.

(a) Explain briefly, giving an example, what is meant by 'evil'? *(2 marks)*

(b) 'Evil is caused by the devil.' What do you think? Explain your opinion. *(3 marks)*

(c) Explain what problems are caused for religious believers by the existence of suffering. *(4 marks)*

(d) Explain briefly some of the ways that religious believers have tried to explain why God allows suffering to happen. *(3 marks)*

(e) 'Evil proves that there is no God.' Do you agree? Give reasons for your answer, showing that you have thought about more than one point of view. Refer to religious arguments in your answer. *(6 marks)*

Examiner's tip

Evaluation questions ask you to 'give reasons for your answer, showing that you have thought about more than one point of view'. You must show that you understand why some people will disagree with your opinions.

4 Immortality

4.1 What is meant by immortality?

A Everyone dies eventually

What is meant by death?

One thing on which everyone agrees is that people die eventually. Death is when a person's physical body stops functioning, and their life on earth in their current physical form ends. The medical profession considers that a person is dead when brain activity stops. Everyone agrees that this is what is meant by death, but not everyone agrees that it is the end. Some people believe that there is survival after death in some way.

Some people argue that death is not the end of life, and that we continue in some form after death. There are many different ideas about the form that survival after death might take. They include:

- the continuation of our genes in our children and their descendants
- the view that we live on in our life's 'work'
- the view that we live on in the memory of others
- the **immortality** of the **soul**
- the **resurrection** of the body
- reincarnation or rebirth.

Key terms

Immortality: endless life or existence; life after death.

Soul: the spiritual rather than physical part of humans.

Resurrection: rising from the dead or returning to life (applied to souls after death).

Case study

William Shakespeare 'lives'?

William Shakespeare died in 1616, but he is probably one of the best known Englishmen in the world. This is because his plays have been translated into all the major languages and have been performed more than those of any other playwright. He is considered the greatest dramatist who has ever lived and, because he is still remembered, many people would argue that he lives on through his works. Shakespeare has no direct descendants and so he has not lived on in the DNA of future generations.

B   *Is Shakespeare immortal because of his plays?*

C   *Do people survive death in the DNA of their children?*

Discussion activity

With a partner, in a group or as a whole class, discuss whether or not survival after death in the genes of one's children is the same as surviving death because one has an immortal soul.

AQA   Examiner's tip

Make sure that you are able to explain the different ways that people believe in life after death.

Activities

1   Explain what is meant by 'death'.

2   Explain **three** different ways in which people might survive their death.

Summary

You should now be able to explain what is meant by death and different ideas about the afterlife.

Ideas of immortality: a legacy, a memory, resurrection

■ Immortality

Immortality is the idea that even though an individual is physically dead, they continue to live on in some way. Two possible ways by which people might achieve immortality are:

- through a **legacy** left as the result of their life's 'work'
- through the memory of others.

Through a legacy

Some people believe that immortality may be achieved through the legacy that the individual leaves behind. This legacy might be a great work of art, music, literature or architecture; a scientific discovery or invention; or some charitable work. For example, Galileo is still remembered for using the telescope to prove that the earth and other planets moved around the sun.

However, once that legacy is gone, such as a building they designed being demolished, the person is no longer remembered through that legacy. Can individuals, therefore, achieve immortality through a legacy?

Research activity 🔍

Andrew Carnegie
Using the internet and/or a library, find out why many libraries and colleges carry the name Carnegie.

Through the memory of others

Some people survive in the memory of family and friends, who probably have photographs, keepsakes and fond recollections of the person who has died. However, when the last person who knew them also dies, then that memory dies with him or her. For a believer, therefore, survival in the memory of others cannot be considered as providing immortality. When believers speak of immortality, they mean life after death.

■ Immortality through resurrection

Some people think immortality is achieved through resurrection. Resurrection is the belief that the person is raised from the dead in some form. This could either be in a physical form or as an immortal soul. The resurrection of the person could take place at death, or at some future date at the end of time called Judgement Day, when some religions teach that everyone will be raised from the dead and judged by God. Judaism, Christianity and Islam all believe in resurrection after death.

Objectives

Investigate what is meant by immortality.

Explore the idea that a legacy, a memory and resurrection are forms of immortality.

Key terms

Legacy: something handed down from an ancestor; a way of being remembered after death.

Heaven: the state of eternal happiness in the presence of God that Christians believe will be granted to the faithful after this life.

Hell: the state of eternal separation from God, seen as punishment for sin.

∞ **links**

Look back to page 74 to remind yourself of the meaning of immortality and soul.

Christian beliefs

Christianity teaches about the resurrection of the body. For many Christians, this is a spiritual body. For others, it is a new, immortal, physical body. Some Christians believe that individuals are raised from the dead and judged by God at death, when they go to either **heaven** or **hell**. Other Christians believe that judgement takes place for everyone on Judgement Day. Catholics believe that individual souls, which will eventually go to heaven, exist first in a state called purgatory where they are cleansed of their sins and made ready for heaven.

Jewish beliefs

Judaism teaches spiritual resurrection. When people die they are resurrected in a shadowy place called Sheol. They wait there for 'the World to come' when God will judge them. God makes people aware not only of the life they lived, but also of the life they could have lived if they had made the right choices. The pain of regret at wrong choices helps to cleanse the person's soul. There is no belief in heaven or hell in Judaism, so the final destination for Jews is one of the seven levels to God. The better the life lived according to God's laws, then the closer the soul gets to God.

Muslim beliefs

Islam teaches that after the body is placed in the grave, the soul is taken for questioning by two angels. Good souls are able to answer the questions but the souls to be punished cannot. The souls wait for Judgement Day when Allah will either send them to Paradise (heaven) or hell. Muslims do not agree about what happens between death and Judgement Day. This period of waiting is called Barzakh. Some Muslims believe that the soul is returned to the grave after questioning, and waits in either comfort or pain according to whether the person was a sinner or not. Other Muslims believe that the souls go to a special place to wait.

A 'Day of Judgement' is the artist Hartmann Schedel's (1440–1514) interpretation of the dead rising to stand before God on Judgement Day

Summary

You should now be able to explain what is meant by resurrection, legacy and survival in the memory of others, and be able to describe and explain religious beliefs about resurrection.

■ Immortality through reincarnation

Some people believe that humans achieve immortality through **reincarnation**. This is the belief that after death the person's soul is transferred into a new body at birth, which may be totally different from that of the previous life. In each reincarnation, the 'soul' lives a different life in a different body. At death, the soul moves (migrates) from the dying body into a new body. This is sometimes called the 'transmigration of souls'. The aim is that, through each lifetime, the soul will improve itself, until it achieves perfection. When it is perfect, the soul will not be reborn but will enter a state of bliss. Hinduism and Sikhism believe in reincarnation. The law of karma is important in judging the quality of each life lived.

Objectives

Explore the ideas of immortality of reincarnation and rebirth.

Key terms

Reincarnation: being born again in another form.

Karma: the law of cause and effect (Hinduism).

Rebirth: being born again after death.

Research activity

The Hindu goddess Kali

Using the internet and/or a library, find out about the role of the goddess Kali in the cycle of death and rebirth.

∞ links

Look back to page 38 for Hindu beliefs about God.

The law of karma

Karma is the acceptance that there is a relationship between what people do and what happens to them. The consequences of an action may not be experienced in this life, but may influence the next. Events that happen to people in the present life may be the result of actions in past lives. Good or bad actions build up good or bad karma. This will influence events in the next life and whether an individual is reborn to a higher or lower situation.

Hindu beliefs

Hindus believe that the soul (atman) is eternal. Their goal is to be united with the Supreme Reality (Brahman) and obtain moksha (release from the cycle of life, death and rebirth (samsara)). People who live in the right way according to their faith achieve good karma. People who disregard the teachings of their faith will build up bad karma, which will influence the quality of their next life. Hindus believe that a reincarnated soul does not carry personal qualities from one life to the next, but the immortal essence of the atman continues into each life.

A *The Hindu God, Shiva, started the cycle of life and death*

Sikh beliefs

Sikhs also believe in reincarnation. The soul remains in the cycle of birth and death until it has become good enough to dwell with God forever, and the cycle of samsara ends. The liberation from the cycle of reincarnation is called mukti. Each life lived depends on the law of karma. The Sikh gurus taught that people move closer to reunion with God or further away from reunion as a result of their karma.

∞ links

Look back to page 39 for Sikh beliefs about God.

As a whole class, discuss the statement: 'If I am in another body, living another life, it cannot be me that has survived.' Do you agree? Give reasons for your answer, showing that you have thought about more than one point of view.

You need to be able to explain the differences between a belief in reincarnation and a belief in rebirth.

Immortality through rebirth

Buddhists prefer to use the term **rebirth** rather than reincarnation. This is because they do not believe people have souls (the Buddhist term 'anatta' means 'no self/no soul'). Reincarnation suggests that there is an immortal soul that continues from one life to the next. The Buddha taught that it is not an individual soul, but an ever-changing individual character, which moves from rebirth to rebirth. The continuity between each life is more cause and effect than the continuation of a soul. This could be considered as the consciousness of the person surviving from life to life. One way to think of it is as a flame being transferred from one candle to another. Each flame is not identical but it is linked to the previous flame. Buddhists accept that each life is linked through the law of karma. The quality of the next life is influenced by the good or bad of the previous ones. Buddhists do not believe in God so there is no union with God at the end of the cycle of rebirth. It is when Buddhists achieve enlightenment that nibbana is reached, that is freedom from suffering and individual existence.

B   A flame transferred from candle to candle is not identical

1 Explain what is meant by 'reincarnation'.
2 Explain what is meant by 'rebirth'.
3 Choose **one** religion that believes in either reincarnation or rebirth, and explain what that religion believes happens after death.

1 Choose between Buddhism, Sikhism or Hinduism. Using the internet and/or a library, research the religion's teaching about reincarnation or rebirth.
2 Write an account of the beliefs about what happens after death of the religion you have chosen.

Summary

You should now be able to explain what is meant by reincarnation and rebirth, and the ideas about karma.

Problems with beliefs about immortality

Problems associated with resurrection

We know that the physical body decays after death, so one problem with resurrection is describing what form the body raised from the dead will take. If there is no separate part of the human body called the 'soul', and an individual is a living, physical body and nothing more, then how can that person be resurrected?

A new improved body

One suggestion is that people are given a new, immortal body when they are resurrected. The body still looks the same as the person who died and has his or her memories, but it is an immortal body that will not age or decay.

The body dies but the soul continues

Some religious believers say that the body decays, but each person has an immortal soul that continues after death. When people die their physical bodies decay in the ground, but their souls are resurrected to an afterlife.

One problem with this is that if people have souls, why is there no evidence of their existence? The medical profession has not found a part of a body matching the concept of a soul. Many believers respond by suggesting that the soul is made of a different substance from the physical body and cannot be seen or detected by medical equipment.

Another problem relates to identity. If people are recognised because of their physical form, can it still be the same person if there is no longer a body? Many believers would answer that people's memories provide their identity. If the soul still has the memories of the life lived, then it is still the same person.

Problems associated with reincarnation and rebirth

Reincarnation and rebirth are different understandings of the cycle of life and death, but both beliefs have the same problems associated with them.

People don't survive death

If people are reincarnated or reborn into a new life when they die, then many people would argue that they have not survived death because they are no longer the same person. If they are living a new life in a new body with different memories, then they are a new person.

Hindus and Sikhs would argue that the immortal soul continues, and therefore what matters from each life continues into the next. Buddhists believe that there is continuity between one life and the next, so life has not ended.

Objectives

Investigate the problems associated with the different options of immortality.

AQA Examiner's tip

Be careful not to confuse similar terms: 'resurrection', 'reincarnation' and 'rebirth'. If you get them muddled, it could cost you marks.

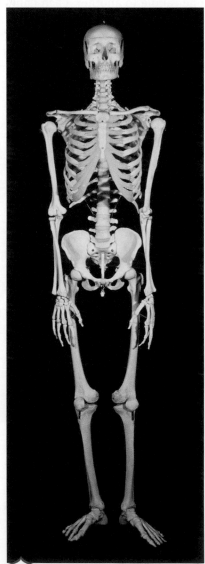

A *We know the body decays after death*

links

Look back to page 10 for the meaning of creation.

Discussion activity

With a partner, in a group or as a whole class, discuss whether or not you can be the same person who died if you get a new improved body.

Extension activity

Using the internet and/or a library find out more about the clinical definition of death.

B Buddhists believe that there is a cycle of birth and death

To be reborn is not the aim

People who aim to be reborn or reincarnated are working towards the total loss of personal identity as they become one with God. They want this to happen. They believe that life consists of hardship and suffering, and to become one with God is the ultimate achievement of complete happiness. At the point when this is achieved, the individual ceases to exist. They are not trying to be reborn.

Memories of past lives

Some people say that the fact that people have memories of past lives is evidence to support reincarnation and rebirth. Historical records have confirmed some of these descriptions of past lives.

Other people ask whether these memories of a former life can be classed as 'proof' of earlier lives or the existence of a soul. Not all of the memories of earlier lives under hypnosis have been found to be accurate. People may be remembering information gained in childhood and mistakenly interpreting this as a past life.

links

The mind/soul/body debate is examined in more detail on pages 90–93.

Research activity

Richard Dawkins

Using the internet and/or a library, find out what the scientist Richard Dawkins believes about the idea of a soul.

Activities

1. a Explain **one** of the problems associated with resurrection.
   b Explain a possible solution to the problem.
2. a Explain **one** of the problems associated with reincarnation.
   b Explain a possible solution to the problem.
3. 'Without a physical body, it is not me who survives death.' Do you agree? Give reasons for your answer, showing you have thought about more than one point of view.

Summary

You should now be able to explain and evaluate the problems associated with the different ideas about immortality.

Evidence of immortality: scriptural accounts and revelation

■ Evidence of immortality

Most religions teach that God has revealed himself through the **scriptural** accounts (holy writings) and believers use these to support their belief in life after death. Religious believers accept that the teachings within the scriptures are true. These teachings form the basis of their religion, including beliefs about life after death. If their religion teaches that there is life after death, then, for the believer, there is life after death.

Buddhism

The Buddhist beliefs about rebirth are based on the teachings of the Buddha. There are many scriptures in Buddhism but the most important is the collection of the Buddha's teachings called the Tripitaka. The Buddha gained enlightenment about how to put an end to suffering and achieve nibbana. If the Buddha's followers wish to do the same, then they must follow his teachings (the Dhamma). The teachings include an explanation of the effects of good and bad karma on the next life.

Christianity

Christians say in the Creed that they believe in 'the resurrection of the body and the life everlasting'. Christians accept that eternal life with God begins when a person accepts the Christian faith, including the resurrection of Jesus. John 11:25–26, quoted in the beliefs and teachings box opposite is read at funerals to remind Christians that eternal life comes through Jesus.

St Paul helped people to understand Christian teaching in his letters, which form part of the New Testament. St Paul taught that Christians will be raised with a new spiritual body after death. Many Christians believe that this body will keep the person's individual identity.

Hinduism

Hindus have many sacred texts to guide them. These include the four Vedas, the Upanishads and the Bhagavad Gita. By following the guidance in the texts, it is hoped that moksha will be achieved.

Islam

Muslims believe that the Qur'an is the direct Word of Allah and, therefore, whatever it says about the resurrection of the body is exactly what will happen. The Qur'an makes it clear that there will be resurrection of the body and judgement by Allah after death.

Judaism

The sacred scriptures of the Jews include the Torah and the Talmud. There are references to God raising people from the dead, and the sorrows of Sheol, but otherwise there is no clear picture of what

---

Objectives

Investigate evidence of immortality from scriptural accounts and revelation.

⬤⬤ links

Look back to pages 76–81 to remind yourself of beliefs about the afterlife.

Key terms

Scripture: the sacred writings of a religion.

⬤⬤ links

Look back to page 30 for what is meant by revelation.

Beliefs and teachings

Jesus said to her, 'I am the resurrection and the life. He who believes in me will live, even though he dies; and whoever lives and believes in me will never die. Do you believe this?'

John 11:25–26

Beliefs and teachings

The kind of seed sown
will produce that kind of fruit.
Those who do good will reap good results.
Those who do evil will reap evil results.
If you carefully plant a good seed,
You will joyfully gather good fruit.

Teaching of the Buddha

Beliefs and teachings

Fix your mind on Me, be devoted to Me, offer service to Me, bow down to Me, and you shall certainly reach Me. I promise you because you are very dear to Me.

Bhagavad Gita

happens after death. This has led to different interpretations in Judaism and different beliefs about the kind of life after death.

Sikhism

The sacred book of the Sikhs is the Guru Granth Sahib. The holy book teaches Sikhs what they must do to break the cycle of reincarnation and to remain with God for ever.

■ The problems

There are several problems in accepting the scriptural accounts and revelations as evidence of immortality. These include the following:

- The scriptural accounts and revelations are accepted as true by the believers in that religion. If people do not belong to that religion, then they are not likely to accept them as true.

- The scriptural accounts and revelations do not agree with each other. They cannot all be right, so they do not provide guidance as to what really happens after death.

- Sometimes the scriptural accounts and revelations lack detail of what people are to believe, and this has led to interpretation of the accounts could be wrong.

- Scriptures originate from a time when there was little knowledge of medical science. Many of the teachings in the scriptures appear to conflict with modern knowledge in science and medicine.

A *Why is this gravestone in the shape of a cross?*

B *Muslims believe that the Qur'an is the actual Word of Allah*

Beliefs and teachings

It is God who gives you life
then gives you death;
then He will gather you together
For the Day of Judgement
About which there is no doubt.

Qur'an 26

Beliefs and teachings

The LORD brings death and
    makes alive;
he brings down to the grave and
    raises up.

1 Samuel 2:6

Beliefs and teachings

Those who meditate on God attain salvation. For them, the cycle of birth and death is eliminated.

Guru Granth Sahib Ji, 11

⃝⃝ links

Any evidence accepted as genuine proof of life after death is also a form of religious experience. Look back to pages 18–19 to remind yourself of the argument from religious experience.

Activities

1 Explain how the evidence from scripture and revelation can be used by some people to prove life after death.

2 Explain why the evidence from scripture and revelation is not accepted as proof of life after death by some people.

3 Read St Paul's first letter to the Corinthians in 1 Corinthians 15:15–29. Explain what St Paul is teaching about life after death.

Summary

You should now be able to explain and evaluate the evidence of immortality from scriptural accounts and revelation.

4.6 Evidence of immortality: experience of ghosts, channelling and near-death experiences

Further evidence of immortality

Besides the support of sacred texts and revelation, there is other evidence to support immortality. This evidence includes:

- experience of ghosts
- **channelling**
- near-death experiences (NDE).

Experience of ghosts

Some people argue that ghosts are genuine manifestations of dead people rather than hallucinations, because often more than one person sees them. There have been sightings at the same place by different people at different times, which would support some sightings as genuine. As ghosts appear to be able to walk through walls, this evidence would support the belief in the resurrection of the body in a spiritual form.

Research activity

Hauntings at Borley Rectory

Borley Rectory is claimed to be the most haunted house in England. Using the internet, find out about the wide variety of sightings seen there, and explanations for and against the ghosts being genuine manifestations.

Channelling

Channelling involves communication between the living and those who have died and are in the spirit world. Many of those (mediums) who claim to be able to contact the dead have passed on messages from departed spirits that contain accurate information, which was previously unknown to the medium. Channelling is believed by some people to be evidence of life after death.

Near-death experiences

Advances in modern technology have resulted in more people who have been declared clinically 'dead' being resuscitated. While 'dead', some patients describe experiences that are very similar. These are called near-death experiences (NDEs). The most common feature is the feeling of being drawn down a tunnel towards a light, a sense of great happiness and the desire not to return. The experiences are so similar, remembered in detail and often life-changing, that they are accepted as evidence of life after death.

Objectives

Investigate evidence of immortality from experience of ghosts, channelling and near-death experiences.

Key terms

Channelling: communicating with the dead through a medium.

Near-death experience (NDE): some people, when they are close to death or in an intense operation situation, claim to have had a sense of themselves leaving their bodies and seeing what exists beyond this life.

A Do ghosts exist?

AQA **Examiner's tip**

Make sure that you are able to answer questions that ask you what is meant by channelling and a near-death experience.

Case study

The experience of a Sikh, Ajit Singh

Ajit was a rich business man. He had a heart attack and found himself looking down at his body. He was drawn along a tunnel towards a beautiful light. He could see dead relatives in the light. He knew that the light was God. He did not want to go back but he was told that it was not his time to die. He re-entered his body and found that he had been resuscitated in hospital. He never forgot the experience and it changed him. He no longer wanted to make money but to help others, and he began to work with the poor.

Extension activity

Using the internet, find out what happened to Pam Reynolds and why her experience is supportive of the NDE as evidence of life after death.

■ The problems

There are several problems in accepting these experiences as evidence of immortality. These problems include the following:

- Ghosts could be hallucinations. It could be a trick of the light, a breath of wind or poor eyesight that causes people to think that they have seen a ghost. It could even be a hoax, where someone has played a trick on people to make them think that they have seen a ghost.

- The investigations of some mediums have proved that they are frauds. Others appear to be genuine, but it might be that they are simply reading the body language of the people to whom they are giving the message.

- NDEs are given that name because the person is not dead. The experience is the result of oxygen starvation that causes hallucinations.

B   *NDEs have been reported from all over the world*

Activities

1   Explain how the evidence from near-death experiences can be used by some people to prove life after death.

2   Explain why the evidence from near-death experiences is not accepted by some people as proof of life after death.

Discussion activity

As a whole class, discuss whether or not the experience of seeing ghosts would provide evidence of immortality.

Summary

You should now be able to explain and evaluate what is meant by evidence of immortality from experiences of ghosts, channelling and near-death experiences.

Argument against immortality: lack of proof

Evidence based on a lack of proof

The major problem in trying to prove immortality is that there is no certainty that anyone has actually come back from the dead, or has contacted the living through a medium. Whatever reasons a religious believer gives as proof of immortality, atheists can counter them with reasons why they cannot be accepted.

A *Cremation destroys the physical body*

Objectives

Investigate the evidence against immortality based on lack of proof.

links

Look back to pages 8–9 to remind yourself of what is meant by proof and how things are proved.

AQA *Examiner's tip*

You need to be able show that you have thought about more than one point of view when answering questions about immortality.

Activities

1 Explain the meaning of the term 'immortality'.

2 How might the work of a medium prove that there is immortality?

Bodies decay in the grave or are burned

People can see for themselves that the bodies of dead people are not everlasting. They have proof that the physical form of humans does not survive death. What they do not have is proof that the deceased receives a new spiritual body or has an immortal soul that leaves the body at death.

Discussion activity

1 Shakespeare described death as 'the undiscovered country, from whose bourn [boundary] no traveller returns'. Discuss what you think Shakespeare meant. Do you agree with his view that no one returns from death? Give reasons for your opinion.

Scriptures and accounts of revelation differ

There are different understandings in scriptures of what life after death is like. Therefore these scriptural accounts and revelations cannot be accepted as proof of immortality.

links

Look back to pages 82–83 to remind yourself of the evidence from scriptural accounts and revelation.

The existence of ghosts, channelling and NDEs cannot be proved

Although there are many people who accept ghosts, channelling and NDEs as proof of immortality, there are many reasons why people argue that there is not enough proof to support them as genuine evidence.

Wishful thinking

All the evidence that religious believers offer as proof of the existence of an afterlife could be no more than wishful thinking. The believers are so eager to have proof of an afterlife to support their religious beliefs that they are willing to accept any 'evidence', however weak.

Also, people fear death and to teach that there is life after death is a comfort to the living.

■ Proof of immortality?

- Most religions argue that there is proof of immortality and that they need no more proof than their faith. They know through faith that what they have been taught about life after death is true.

- A philosopher called John Hick argued that there is proof available to support life after death. Unfortunately, this proof is only available when we die, as when we die we will know that there is an afterlife.

 links

Look back to pages 84–85 to remind yourself of the evidence from ghosts, channelling and NDEs.

Discussion activity

2 With a partner, discuss whether finding out that there is an afterlife after you are dead can be considered as proof of immortality.

Research activity

John Hick

Using the internet, find out more about John Hick's reasons for supporting the idea that there is life after death.

B *Muslims are certain that there is life after death*

Activity

3 'I believe in God and that is all the proof that is needed to support the existence of immortality.' Do you agree? Give reasons for your answer, showing that you have thought about more than one point of view.

Summary

You should now be able to evaluate whether or not there is sufficient proof to support immortality.

Argument against immortality: from science and atheism

Evidence from science

Many philosophers and scientists argue that modern science has shown that there are links between the brain and the body and, therefore, that the mind/soul cannot survive on its own. Scientific theories that could count against immortality are:

- the theory of evolution
- the use of cryonics
- exploration of space.

Each person is a product of evolution

The atheist and scientist Richard Dawkins rejects any concept of an immortal soul. Dawkins claims that the belief in the soul is the result of people refusing to accept that there is no purpose to life. He believes that each human is the product of evolution, and people only survive by passing their DNA on to future generations. Dawkins believes that scientific findings have shown that humanity is no more than DNA carried to ensure the survival of the species. Morality is there to make sure that mistakes are not repeated, and that society is protected.

Objectives

Investigate evidence against immortality from science and atheism.

AQA **Examiner's tip**

Make sure that you are able to answer questions asking what is meant by 'evolution'.

∞ **links**

Look back to pages 14–15 to remind yourself of the theory of evolution.

Discussion activity

1 In his book, *River Out of Eden* (1995), Richard Dawkins said, 'There is no spirit-driven life force, no throbbing, heaving, pullulating, protoplasmic, mystic jelly. Life is just bytes and bytes and bytes of digital information.'

As a whole class, discuss what you think Dawkins meant.

Religious believers would respond that people may have evolved but that still does not deny the possibility of a soul. Buddhists, Hindus and Sikhs believe that they are going through a cycle of birth and death until they reach a state of perfection. Some people might consider this a form of evolution.

The use of cryonics

Cryonics is the low-temperature preservation of humans, who can no longer be kept alive by modern medicine, until such time as resuscitation (reviving a body from an unconscious state) and a cure may be possible. The US baseball player, Ted Williams, is one of the famous people frozen in the hope of being woken up at some future date. If people die and are frozen with the possibility of being brought back to life, then their afterlife will be spent in this world.

Resuscitation is deemed impossible by members of most religions. Only God can resurrect the dead, and once the soul has left the body, it cannot be retrieved. However, this raises a question: at what point does the soul leave the body? Is it at the moment of death or is it at

Extension activity

Using the internet and/or a library, find out more about cryonics.

some later date such as the Day of Judgement? Believers are not in agreement as to when this happens. If it is at some point before the body is resuscitated, then the question is raised as to whether the soul would be returned to it, or would it be a body without a soul? These are questions to which believers would provide different answers.

The exploration of space

Since the late 1950s, satellites have been sent into space; and since the 1960s humans have gone into space. Today, telescopes can see into the farthest galaxies. If there is an afterlife, then surely some evidence would have been seen of the souls of the dead becoming one with the universe or going to heaven. As no such evidence has been seen, then there cannot be survival after death.

Many religious believers would point out that the immortal soul must be of a different substance to the physical body or it exists as a spiritual being. Therefore, one would not expect to see evidence of it. Also, the experience of going into space has converted many astronauts to a belief in God. James Irwin who walked on the moon in 1971 said, 'I felt the power of God as I'd never felt it before.'

A *Many astronauts have become theists after going into space*

■ The view of atheists

The arguments against immortality support the atheist's view that there is no God and no survival after death. Some atheists would say that life is without purpose. Others, such as Humanists, respond by attaching prime importance to human matters and to improving the quality of people's life on earth.

Religious believers would point out that if there is no divine purpose to life, why do so many people put effort into worship and into making life better for others? People's desire to worship in itself suggests that atheists are wrong – there is a purpose to life and that purpose includes achieving eternal life with God on earth and in a life after death. Many would argue that in serving others, one is able to get closer to God.

Discussion activity

2 As a whole class, discuss the atheist's view that there is no God and no survival after death. Give reasons for your answer, showing that you have thought about more than one point of view.

B *If there is no divine purpose to life, why do so many people have religious beliefs?*

Activities

1 Explain how science can be used against immortality.

2 Explain why atheists reject immortality.

Summary

You should now be able to explain and evaluate evidence against immortality from science and atheism.

4.9 Dualism

What is materialism?

Materialism is the belief that our minds are inseparable from our bodies. Materialists reject any idea of survival of a soul once the physical body is dead. Materialist reasons for not accepting survival after death are:

- life depends on a functioning brain, nervous system and physical body
- death involves the destruction of the brain, the nervous system and physical body.

Therefore, a person's life ends at death, as life cannot continue without a physical form.

Materialists consider that there is no scientific evidence for the existence of a soul, and that it will never be possible to prove whether or not a soul exists. They argue that modern science has shown that there are links between the brain and the body, and that the mind therefore cannot survive on its own. Materialism is the opposite view to **dualism**.

Objectives

Know and understand the concept of dualism.

Key terms

Dualism: the idea that humans have two basic natures, the physical and the spritual.

Extension activity

Using the internet and/or a library, find out more about materialism and what a materialist believes about life after death.

Discussion activity

With a partner, in a group or as a whole class, discuss whether it is possible to believe in both materialism and life after death? Give reasons for your answer, showing that you have thought about more than one point of view.

A *Is the mind separate from the body?*

Mind or soul?

Some people use mind and soul to mean the same thing. Other people would describe the mind as the thinking, feeling part of a human, and the soul the spiritual part of a person.

Research activity

Plato and the soul

Plato (c.428–348 BCE) was an Ancient Greek philosopher. Using the internet and/or a library, find out what Plato believed about the body, soul and mind.

What is dualism?

Dualists argue that there are two distinct parts to a person: a mind (soul) and body. A dualist approach to mind and body argues that the mind determines our personality and the body is an outer shell for our real self. The body will decay, but the mind/soul, associated with the higher realities such as truth, goodness and justice, is immortal. Dualists argue that the mind/soul is separate from the physical body, although while a person is alive the two are linked.

The dualism of René Descartes

René Descartes (1596–1650) was a French philosopher, physicist and mathematician. He was also a dualist. Descartes argued that, although it is possible philosophically to doubt the existence of our bodies, we cannot doubt the existence of our minds because we have individual thoughts – 'I think therefore I am.' Even if we are dreaming, we must still exist to have thoughts. Descartes decided that the physical body and the mind/soul must be made of different substances. Our physical body takes up space and can be seen, but the mind/soul must be of a substance that does not take up space and can change shape, position and movement. It cannot be seen with the human eye.

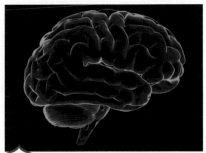

B   *Does the brain contain a soul?*

The physical body and the mind/soul are connected while we are alive. For example, the mind can plan a design but it is the physical body that completes the design. At death, the two separate: the body decays but the soul moves on to the afterlife.

Activities

1   Explain what is meant by 'materialism'.
2   Explain what is meant by 'dualism'.

Summary

You should now be able to know about, and explain, the concept of dualism.

The impact of dualism on the definition of death

Dualism goes along with a definition of death as the moment when the physical body decays and the immortal soul continues. Therefore, dualism agrees with some religious ideas about life after death, but not all.

Some religious believers disagree with dualism because it argues for a separate body and mind/soul. Many Christians, Muslims and Jews believe that the physical body, as well as the soul, will be resurrected, although this body may be in a new spiritual form. They believe that God/Allah has created humans as a unity of mind, body and soul, and that people keep their own identity when they die. The soul is not a separate substance from the body but it is the 'spark' from God/Allah that gives life to the physical body.

Objectives

Investigate the impact of the concept of dualism on how death is defined.

Investigate the issues raised by dualism.

AQA Examiner's tip

Make sure that you are able to explain the concept of dualism.

A *'The LORD God formed the man from the dust of the ground and breathed into his nostrils the breath of life, and the man became a living being' (Genesis 2:7)*

> *Now that the soul is what makes our body live; so the soul is the primary source of all these activities that differentiate levels of life: growth, sensation, movement, understanding.*
>
> Aquinas, *Summa Theologica*

The combinations of body and soul

This chapter has considered different beliefs about life after death, and the challenges to these beliefs. Buddhists do not believe in a soul as such.

Hindus and Sikhs agree that in each life the body and soul come together, but this state cannot continue after death as the soul or essence of the person begins a new life in a new body.

Extension activity

St Thomas Aquinas

Using the internet, find out more about St Thomas Aquinas's beliefs about the existence of a soul.

∞ links

Look back to page 79 for Buddhist beliefs about anatta and life after death.

Christians, Jews and Muslims believe that God/Allah created the whole person, and that it is the whole person who is raised after death. They have to overcome the problem of a body's decay after death. One solution mentioned is that at death people receive a new body.

If the resurrection of the body does not happen until Judgement Day, then the problem is solved by the belief that God/Allah reunites the body and soul at that time. After death, the soul waits to be resurrected with its physical body. Christians, Jews and Muslims believe God/Allah created humans from dust or clay originally and so it is just as easy for God/Allah to recreate them on Judgement Day. God/Allah is capable of anything.

∞ links

Look back to pages 76–79 to remind yourself of the different religious beliefs about life after death.

Beliefs and teachings

Man thinks that, We shall not assemble his bones.

Yes Truly! We are able to restore his very fingers!

Qur'an 75:3–4

B *There is a belief that God will reunite people's souls and bodies on Judgement Day*

Activities

1 Explain why a belief in dualism might be a problem for some religious believers.

2 Explain why some religious believers accept the resurrection of the body after death.

Summary

You should now be able to explain and evaluate the concept of dualism, and the different views that believers hold about dualism.

Research activity 🔍

Judgement Day

Choose either Christianity, Judaism or Islam and, using the internet, find out more about the religion's beliefs about Judgement Day.

4

AQA **Examiner's tip**

Remember, you may refer to one or more than one religion or denomination in the examination.

Immortality – summary

For the examination you should now be able to:

✔ understand what is meant by 'immortality'

✔ explain the terms 'resurrection', 'reincarnation', 'rebirth' and 'dualism'

✔ evaluate the evidence for and against evidence for immortality, including: scriptural accounts, revelation, ghost experiences, channelling, near-death experiences, lack of proof, science and atheism

✔ evaluate the impact of dualism on the concept of death.

Sample answer

1 Write an answer to the following examination question:

'Near-death experiences are hallucinations.' Do you agree? Give reasons for your answer, showing you have thought about more than one point of view. Refer to religious arguments in your answer. *(6 marks)*

2 Read the following sample answer:

> I agree that near-death experiences are hallucinations because when someone is very ill and near to death, their brain may be starved of oxygen. This is what causes the sensation some people describe as leaving their bodies. They may think they have gone to heaven and met God, but they did not really. When they say they know what was going on while they were supposed to be dead, it is because they could still hear what was going on around them. They are near death, but not actually dead.
>
> Other people would not agree with me. They do not think near-death experiences are hallucinations, but the person's soul left their body and went down a tunnel to a beautiful light. They believe this because they believe in an afterlife and think that too many people have had it happen to them for it not to be true. People who have had such an experience often change their life and are no longer frightened of dying.

3 With a partner, discuss the sample answer. Do you think that there are other things that the student could have included in the answer?

4 What mark would you give this answer out of 6? (Look at the mark scheme in the Introduction on page 7 (AO2) before you attempt this.) What are the reasons for the mark you have given?

AQA Examination-style questions

1 Look at the drawings and answer the following questions.

I believe that we are resurrected after death.

I believe in rebirth after death.

I believe in reincarnation.

(a) What is meant by the term 'immortality'? (2 marks)

(b) Explain, using examples, the difference between reincarnation and resurrection. (4 marks)

(c) 'We need a body if we are to survive after death.' What do you think? Explain your opinion. (3 marks)

(d) Explain briefly the reasons some people might give for not believing in life after death. (3 marks)

(e) 'There is plenty of evidence to prove that there is an afterlife.' Do you agree? Give reasons for your answer, showing that you have thought about more than one point of view. Refer to religious arguments in your answer. (6 marks)

Examiner's tip

Remember that when you are given a statement and asked 'do you agree?' you must show what you think and the reasons why other people might take a different view. If your answer is one-sided, you can only achieve a maximum of 4 marks. If you make no comment about religious belief or practice, you will achieve no more than 3 marks.

5 Miracles

5.1 Introduction to miracles

Theists use the term 'miracle' to refer to 'an event performed by God that appears to break the laws of nature'. Some such miracles involve healing. Not all religious believers accept that miracles occur. Religious believers who accept the existence of miracles think that God performs them to teach people something about God, or to help them have greater faith.

Do Buddhists believe in miracles?

Buddhists do not believe in God, and think that everything happens through cause and effect (karma). There is a debate within Buddhism as to whether miracles occur at all. An event that appears to be miraculous may actually be caused by someone as the result of the stage of enlightenment they have reached.

■ Examples of miracles

In those religions that do accept the existence of miracles, there are many examples of people being healed and some examples of people being raised from the dead. There are also miracles in which an event occurs that would normally be thought impossible, such as the sun standing still or someone walking on water. Miracles are often linked to a holy person or place thought to be holy by followers of the religion.

Objectives

Investigate what is meant by the term 'miracle'.

⚭ links

Look back to pages 16–17 at the argument from miracles for the existence of God. It will be helpful to read this section before you begin this chapter on miracles.

Activity

Read the account of Jesus healing the paralysed man in the New Testament (Mark 2:1–12). Use your own words to describe what happened.

Case study

The miracle of the milk-drinking statue

On 21 September 1995, a miracle happened at a Hindu temple in India that was shown on television throughout the world. The events began when a Hindu man dreamed that the god, Ganesha, wanted a drink of milk. He went to his local temple and told the priest, who offered a spoonful of milk to the mouth of the stone image of Ganesha. To their surprise the milk disappeared. News spread throughout India of the event and people came from all over. Whenever a spoonful of milk was offered to the image, the milk disappeared. The event was filmed and shown worldwide on television.

 Did Ganesha drink the milk or is there another explanation?

B   *What does the incident of Guru Nanak and the buffalo teach a believer?*

Case study

Guru Nanak and the grazing buffalo

One of the miracles linked to the life of the founder of Sikhism, Guru Nanak, happened when he was a boy. His father sent him to graze the buffalo in the field. While the buffalo were eating the grass, Guru Nanak began to meditate, and forgot to watch the buffalo. They strayed into the next field and ate the crops growing there. The farmer who owned the field was very angry and went to see Guru Nanak's father. When the two men returned together, they found that the crops had not only regrown but were blossoming.

C   *There are many miracles associated with Guru Nanak*

Summary

You should now be able to define what is meant by a miracle.

What is meant by a miracle?

What is a miracle?

A miracle can be defined as an act of God that causes a good outcome. On page 16, it was suggested that there were two types of miracle: miracles that break the **laws of nature**; and miracles that are happy coincidences. In this section, we are going to look at these two types of miracles in more detail.

Miracles that break the laws of nature

These are events that do not normally occur in nature, that break the laws of science as we know them.

For example, Christians and Jews accept a miracle linked to the Israelite leader, Joshua, in which the sun stands still. The sun standing still is not a natural occurrence. According to the book of Joshua, God made the sun stand still at Joshua's request, to give the Jews time to defeat their enemies in battle.

Objectives

Investigate different understandings of what is meant by the term 'miracle'.

Key terms

Laws of nature: descriptions of how scientists expect nature to work.

A *Normally, the sun does not stand still*

Discussion activity

1 With a partner, discuss the reasons why Christians and Jews would argue that God sent a miracle to help Joshua.

Beliefs and teachings

So the sun stood still,
and the moon stopped,
till the nation avenged itself on its enemies,
as it is written in the Book of Jashar.
The sun stopped in the middle of the sky and delayed going down about a full day. There has never been a day like it before or since, a day when the LORD listened to a man. Surely the LORD was fighting for Israel!

Joshua 10:13–14

Activity

1 Read Joshua 10:13–14. Write a description of the miracle.

Other miracles in this category are those that break the laws of nature because of the speed at which the event happens. For example, people declared dead who are then resuscitated following medical intervention. People do naturally recover from illness over a period of time, but in this type of miracle the person suddenly returns to life or is cured.

Miracles that are happy coincidences

These types of miracle do not break the laws of nature, but a coincidence occurs at exactly the right time to bring about a good outcome. It is a coincidence when two people say the same thing at the same time, or turn up wearing the same outfit to a party, but it is not a miracle. For a coincidence to be a miracle, some misfortune has to be prevented or some good achieved. An example is the miracle of stairwell B, in which 16 people survived the collapse of the North Tower of the World Trade Center. Another example would be a parachutist surviving because he lands safely in a tree after his parachute has failed to open.

B *If a parachutist survives when his parachute does not open, is this a miracle?*

Miracles are acts of God

Many people believe that miracles can only be performed by God because only God is outside time and space, and therefore not limited by the laws of nature. If people perform miracles, then most religious believers think it is because God is working through them. Muslims accept the miracles of Jesus but they believe that it was God working through Jesus, and not Jesus himself, who performed them. We will look at this topic in more detail later in the chapter.

AQA Examiner's tip

Make sure that you have examples of the two types of miracles that you can use to support your answers in the examination.

∞ links

Look back to page 16 to read about the miracle of stairwell B.

Discussion activity

2 As a whole class, discuss whether or not happy coincidences can ever be miracles. Give reasons for your answer, showing that you have thought about more than one point of view.

Extension activity

Using the internet and /or a library, find more examples of the two types of miracle.

Summary

You should now be able to explain some different understandings of the term 'miracle'.

Activities

2 Explain, with examples, the **two** types of miracle that religious believers accept.

3 Explain what is meant by describing a miracle as an act of God.

Does God work in the world through miracles?

■ Different views about God working in the world through miracles

One of the questions that many religious believers ask is, 'Does God work in the world through miracles?' Many religious believers accept that a miracle happens when God works in the world in an unusual way: either to show his power, or to show his approval of someone speaking or acting on God's behalf.

Buddhists and atheists reject miracles from God

Buddhists and atheists would agree that God does not work in the world through miracles because Buddhists and atheists do not believe in God. This does not mean that Buddhists reject the concept of miracles, but they do not accept that miracles are the result of an action by God.

Christian beliefs

Christians believe that God works in the world directly through miracles. They believe that Jesus performed miracles that showed the power or love of God, or revealed that Jesus was God in human form. Jesus's miracles included walking on water, healing the sick and raising the dead.

Objectives

Investigate whether or not God works in the world through miracles.

AQA Examiner's tip

Remember that Buddhists do not believe in God and therefore reject miracles as coming from God.

Extension activity

Using the internet and/or a library, find a miracle linked to the life of the Buddha and write an account of what happened.

A In Hinduism, it is believed that miracles are performed by the gods

Hindu beliefs

Hindus believe that some miracles are the result of direct intervention by Brahman, but others are performed by the gods in their many aspects of Brahman, such as Krishna and Rama, or Ganesha drinking milk.

◯◯links

Look back to page 96 to remind yourself of the miracle of Ganesha drinking milk.

Jewish beliefs

Jews believe that God works directly in the world, particularly for the benefit of the Jews. An example of God's intervention occurred when the prophet Moses was leading the Israelites out of Egypt. When they reached the sea, they were trapped and the Egyptians were catching up with them. God parted the Red Sea and the Jews were able to cross safely. As the Egyptians tried to follow, the water closed over them.

B   *The Bible teaches that God performed miracles through the prophet Moses*

Islam

Muslims believe that only Allah can perform miracles. No human can perform miracles, but Allah can work through individuals to perform miracles. Allah performed miracles through all the prophets, to prove that they were chosen by Allah. Muslims accept Jesus as a prophet and that Allah performed miracles through Jesus to show that Jesus was chosen by him. The greatest miracle in Islam is the living Qur'an, sent by Allah as a complete revelation for all time and to all people.

Sikhism

Sikhs believe that miracles occur, and the saints and prophets could perform miracles if they chose. However, they also believe that miracles should not be performed to prove a prophet's power or to gain popularity, or even to prove the greatness or truth of a religion. Miracles should only be used to assist other people, especially to help them understand the right way to live and to believe in God.

Discussion activity 👤👤👤

Sikhs argue that miracles are a cheap way of winning support and can do more harm than good. Discuss this point of view with a partner. What are the reasons for your opinions?

⬭ links

The term 'revelation' is defined and covered in more detail on page 30, or you can look it up in the Glossary at the back of this book.

Activity

'God does not perform miracles in the world.' Do you agree? Give reasons for your answer, showing that you have thought about more than one point of view.

Summary

You should now be able to explain the different understandings in the religions studied about whether or not God works in the world through miracles.

Religious beliefs about humans performing miracles

The previous section discussed different religious attitudes to God working in the world through miracles. In this section, we are going to think about whether or not humans perform miracles. The majority of religious believers think that if humans do perform miracles, then it is only because God is working through them. Other believers think that it is possible for humans to perform miracles without God's intervention.

Miracles in Buddhism

Buddhists who accept that miracles happen think they are performed by humans. However, many Buddhists do not believe that there are such things as miracles. They argue that what is happening is not a miracle but evidence that our knowledge about the world is incomplete. The unexplained event is just something that we cannot yet understand. For example, in the past, illness was thought to be caused by evil spirits or a punishment for sin, but today the causes of disease are generally understood.

Other Buddhists agree that miracles are outside what we observe and know about nature, but believe that they occur through the power of the human mind. They believe that through meditation and leading a moral life, an individual can develop miraculous powers. The Buddha had these powers – he was able to be seen in several places at once, fly through the air, hear things over long distances, read people's minds, walk on hot coals and remember past lives. The ability of a human to perform miracles is not proof that the person is holy. For Buddhists, the purpose of miracles is to benefit others by encouraging them to seek enlightenment because miracles demonstrate what can be achieved by developing the powers of the mind.

Miracles in Hinduism

Hindu beliefs about people's ability to perform miracles are similar to Buddhism, except that Hindus do believe in God, Brahman. Hindus believe that through a positive attitude to life, it is possible to obtain some of the positive energy of the universe. When a Hindu achieves perfection, they gain spiritual or mental powers. These powers enable the individual to perform actions such as to levitate (rise physically off the ground), predict the future, make objects appear and remember past lives.

Hindus believe that miracles are actions of nature which are not understood fully by the observer. Miracles are not supernatural events; they are simply events that the person does not understand, or cannot explain.

Objectives

Investigate whether a human can perform miracles.

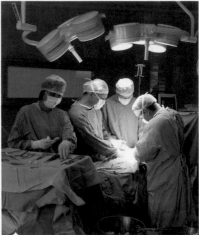

A   *In the past, illness was thought to be caused by evil spirits or sin*

B   *Buddhist monks are able to walk on hot coals. Is this a miracle?*

Miracles in Sikhism

In Sikhism, prophets and saints are able to perform miracles, but this ability should not be used to achieve selfish ends. For example, miracles should not be performed because a king or leader demands them. Guru Arjan and Guru Teg Bahadur underwent tortures and martyrdom rather than perform miracles. When the Sikh gurus performed miracles, they were to help someone or to help a person understand the right way to live and worship.

∞ links

Make sure that you understand the views of the religion(s) you are studying about God working in the world through miracles by reading pages 100–101.

Extension activity

Using the internet and/or a library, find out more about the martyrdoms of Guru Arjan Sahib and Guru Teg Bahadur.

■ Miracles in Christianity, Islam and Judaism

These three religions argue that humans can perform miracles, but only because God works through them. A human is unable to perform miracles without God's help. Some Christians believe that Jesus could perform miracles because he was God on earth in human form. Other Christians believe that because Jesus was closer to God than any other human being, God worked through him as through others, but to a much greater extent. Muslims and Jews believe that only Allah/God can perform miracles, although he may perform them through his chosen prophets.

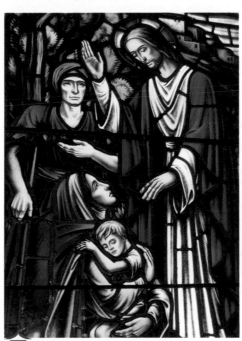

C *Jesus – a miracle worker*

Activity

'Only God can perform miracles.' Do you agree? Give reasons for your answer, showing that you have thought about more than one point of view.

AQA   Examiner's tip

Make sure that you understand the difference between God performing a miracle through a human, and a human performing the miracle.

Summary

You should now be able to discuss different religious beliefs about humans performing miracles.

Examples of miracles from scripture and tradition

All the religions studied have miracles within their **scripture** and/or **tradition**. There are often miracles associated with the birth of the founder of the religion, and holy people within the faith.

Example from Buddhism

Miracles in Buddhism are mainly linked to the traditions associated with the Buddha.

Case study

The Buddha tames an elephant

The Buddha's cousin, Devadatta, was jealous of the Buddha and tried on many occasions to kill him. One day, Devadatta released a fierce and dangerous elephant, Nelagiri, to trample the Buddha. The crazed elephant ran into the town towards the Buddha. A frightened woman accidentally dropped her baby in the path of the elephant. As the animal was about to trample the child, the Buddha calmly touched the elephant's forehead. The elephant stopped and became calm. It then knelt down before the Buddha.

A *The Buddha stopped the elephant Nelagiri from killing a baby*

Example from Hinduism

Many miracles are recorded in the various Hindu scriptures and traditions. These are usually linked to the gods and show their power.

Case study

The birth of Krishna

King Kamsa was told that the eighth son of his sister, Devaki, would grow up to kill him. He imprisoned his sister, and each time she gave birth killed her child. When her eighth child, Krishna, was born, the god Vishnu appeared and told her husband to take the baby and exchange it with a girl born at the same time. As Krishna's father carried him through the prison, the prison doors opened to free him and all the guards remained asleep. When he reached the river, it parted and he was able to reach the palace where a new-born baby girl had been born to the Queen. Everyone in the palace slept as he swapped the babies and took the girl back to the prison. When Kansa heard of the birth of the eighth child, he went to kill the child. When he grabbed the child and threw it against the prison wall, the child flew up to the sky and became a goddess. Krishna survived and grew up in his new home.

B *Krishna was saved as a baby through a miracle*

Example from Islam

In Islam, the scripture, the Qur'an, is a living miracle as it is the direct guide from Allah to each individual, regardless of who they are. Within the scripture there are miracles, many of which are also found in the Christian New Testament associated with Jesus. For example, as in the Christian tradition, Jesus is believed to have been born to a virgin, Mary. In both scriptures, she is told by an angel that she is going to have a baby.

links

Look back to page 101 to learn why the Qur'an is regarded as a miracle by Muslims.

Beliefs and teachings

She said: 'My Lord! How can I have a son when no man has touched me?'

He said, 'God thus creates what He wills: To have anything done When He has decreed a matter He has only to say to it "Be" and it is!'

Qur'an 3:47

There are also miracles associated within the traditions of Islam, especially about the founder of Islam, Muhammad. For example, when he was nearly three, it is believed that two angels entered the camp site, opened Muhammad's chest, removed his heart, cleansed it of sin and then returned it without the child suffering any ill effects.

links

Look back to page 97 to remind yourself of the miracle of Guru Nanak and the buffalo.

Example from Judaism and Christianity

The Christian Old Testament contains the same scriptural accounts of miracles as the Jewish Tenakh. Two famous miracles found in these scriptures are the parting of the Red Sea by Moses to aid the Hebrew slaves escape from Egypt, and the collapse of the walls of Jericho at the right moment to give victory to the Hebrews.

Activity

Read Joshua 5:13–6:27. Write an account of the miraculous collapse of the walls of Jericho.

C   *Sikhs believe that the Guru Granth Sahib is a living guru*

Example from Sikhism

The Guru Granth Sahib is the spiritual authority in Sikhism, available as guidance for all. This scripture is believed to be a miracle in itself and considered to be a living guru. There are also many miracles associated with the Ten Gurus, particularly Guru Nanak.

Discussion activity

As a whole class, consider other possible explanations for these examples of miracles. If you can provide a possible explanation, discuss whether this means that the incident was not a miracle.

AQA   Examiner's tip

Make sure that you have examples of miracles from scripture and tradition to support your answers.

Summary

You should now be able to provide examples of miracles from religious scriptures and traditions.

Examples of miracles from history and personal experience

Examples of miracles from history

Miracles linked to the founders of religions may be considered miracles from history. Miracles throughout history have been used to support the truth of the religion's teachings. These miracles happened in the past and are therefore miracles from history, as are miracles linked to holy people in the religions. In Islam, the Qur'an is considered to be a miracle because this revelation from Allah is relevant to all people throughout history. In all the religions there are many events throughout history, after their scriptures were written, that are thought to have been miracles.

Objectives

Examine examples of miracles from history and personal experience.

⚭ links

Look back to pages 96–105 to remind yourself of examples of miracles.

A *Hindu pilgrims journey to Varanasi in the hope of a miracle cure*

Case study

Miracles associated with Varanasi

Varanasi is one of the most important places of pilgrimage for Hindus. It is where the god Shiva is supposed to have lived, and has been a centre of religious teaching for centuries. Hindus enter the river Ganges at the site and many hope when they bathe in the water that their sins will be miraculously washed away. Other Hindus bathe in the Ganges in the hope of miracle cures.

Miracles often seem to occur at great times of trouble for people and nations, particularly during times of war. During the First World War, British soldiers at Mons believed they owed their lives to a miracle.

B *Jesus performed miracles in the New Testament*

Case study

The Angels of Mons

The miracle of the Angels of Mons occurred at a time when the British Army was in retreat. In August 1914, a group of three angels appeared in the sky to protect the British army during the battle of Mons. Many British soldiers claimed to have seen them. As a result, the British soldiers were given hope and survived.

■ Examples of miracles from personal experience

People are most often convinced of the existence of miracles by extraordinary events that they experience or see for themselves. One of the ways in which people have such an experience is through faith healing.

Research activity ⌕

Miracles in history

Using the internet and/or a library, find some more examples of miracles throughout history.

C   *Can people be cured through the laying on of hands?*

Faith healing is an attempt to cure people or improve health through spiritual means. In some religions, there are acts of worship that include faith healing, or it may be that believers go on pilgrimage to sacred places in the hope of a cure. Prayer, mental practices and spiritual insights are all part of faith healing. Sometimes the cure is gradual and at other times it is sudden.

AQA   **Examiner's tip**

Make sure that you have examples of miracles from history and experience to support your answers.

Extension activity

Using the internet and/or a library, find out more about Lourdes as a place of pilgrimage and healing.

Summary

You should now be able to provide examples of miracles from history and experience.

Evidence of and for miracles

Evidence of miracles

Those who believe in miracles, use the evidence *of* miracles to prove that they have happened:

- Many people see the miracles happening. For example, some think the miracle of the god, Ganesha, drinking milk is strong evidence of miracles, as the miracle was seen worldwide on television. There are many other examples of miracles linked with religious artefacts. For example, a statue of the Virgin Mary has been seen crying blood in a church in Mexico. The priest cleans the statue and wipes away the stains only to see them reappear.

- People experience a miracle for themselves. This is evidence of miracles for the person involved, and for those who see the effect the miracle has on the person. For example, if a person is cured of a terminal illness after doctors have given up hope, this is regarded as evidence of a miracle.

- Miracles are associated with the founders of a religion. These miracles were seen by many people and recorded at the time.

Objectives

Investigate the evidence of and for miracles.

links

Look back to page 96 to remind yourself of the miracle of the god Ganesha drinking milk.

AQA Examiner's tip

Make sure that you understand the difference between evidence *of* miracles and evidence *for* miracles.

Activity

1 Write an explanation of the evidence for miracles in your own words. Support your points with specific examples.

A There have been various miracles linked to statues of the Virgin Mary

Extension activity

Using the internet, find out about the statue of the Virgin Mary seen crying in the church in Akita City, Japan.

■ Evidence for miracles

People who believe in miracles also have reasons *for* accepting miracles as genuine, reasons for believing that they happen:

- There have been too many accounts of miracles for at least some of them not to have happened.
- Miracles are not just events from the past; but still occur today.
- Many miracles have been investigated and no scientific explanation for them can be found.
- The miracles performed by the founders of the religions and other holy people convince people to convert to, and even die for, the religion. If the miracles were not genuine, these people would not have become followers of the religion.
- There have been several research programmes into the power of prayer to heal. The results support the belief that prayer helps to cure people.

B *There is evidence that prayer works*

Case study

The power of prayer to heal

In 1995, a research project began to investigate the power of prayer to heal people. Twenty Aids patients were enrolled in the programme. All patients received the same medical care, but psychic healers prayed for 10 of them. The 10 patients prayed for did not know that they had been chosen. The healers lived over 1,500 miles away from the hospital. During the six-month study, four patients died, but none of them was in the group that was prayed for. At the end of the six months, all the patients prayed for were still alive. The research showed that those not prayed for spent 68 days in hospital and received treatment for 35 Aids-related illnesses. The group prayed for spent only 10 days in hospital and contracted 13 Aids-related illnesses.

Discussion activity

As a whole class, discuss the evidence of or for miracles. Suggest other explanations for the evidence if you do not think they are genuine miracles.

Activities

2 List and explain examples of the evidence *of* miracles a religious believer could use.

3 List and explain the evidence religious believers use *for* believing in miracles.

Summary

You should now be able to explain the evidence of and for miracles.

The power of miracles in revealing God

■ What might be revealed by miracles?

Some religious believers think that miracles reveal qualities of God, as well as providing evidence for his existence. Some of these qualities include:

- God's love and care for his creation, his benevolence
- God's immanence
- God's knowledge and power.

Love and care for his creation

Most religions teach that God created the universe and the world in which humans live. The very act of creation is a miracle and an act of love.

Muslims believe that God's love for his creation is shown through the miracle of the Qur'an as a guide on how to live as God wishes. Christians believe that God's love is shown through the miraculous events linked to Jesus, especially the Resurrection.

Objectives

Investigate the power of miracles in revealing God.

A *Many religions believe the creation of the world is a miracle*

∞ links

Look back to pages 30–31 if you are not sure what is meant by a revelation. The terms 'benevolence' and 'immanence' are also defined and covered in more detail in Chapter 2, or you can look them up in the Glossary at the back of this book.

B *Christians believe that God's love was shown through the miracle of the Resurrection*

Beliefs and teachings

For God so loved the world that he gave his one and only Son, that whoever believes in him shall not perish but have eternal life.

John 3:16

Miraculous healings, for example, might be taken as signs that point to the existence of a loving God. The miracles not only assist people but also help people learn something about God.

AQA *Examiner's tip*

Make sure that you can explain, using examples, the different types of miracle.

∞ links

Look back to pages 40–41 to be certain you understand what is meant by God's immanence.

Immanence

Miracles are believed to show that God is active in the world, and therefore show that God is immanent. Sometimes God performs the miracles directly, as when the waters were parted to allow the Israelites to escape into the desert. These types of miracle show how God controls events. Christians believe that God came into the world as Jesus to save them and that the miracles Jesus performed are evidence of this.

In Hinduism, the gods take human form to rescue the world from chaos or to help people, and use miracles for this purpose.

○○ links

Look back to pages 96–108 for examples of miracles.

Research activity 🔍

Miracles by the founders

Choose **two** of the following people/god and find examples of miracles associated with them:

- Saint Peter
- Elijah
- Guru Nanak
- Krishna

Miracles accepted by other religions, such as Islam and Judaism, show that God works in the world indirectly. When God performs the miracle through a person, such as a founder of the religion, he is supporting the individual's claim, or showing some of his love or power through the person.

C   *There are miracles associated with St Peter*

Knowledge and power

Miracles believed to break the laws of nature show that God is able to interfere with the natural workings of the world. God is not just working outside the laws of nature. He is changing those laws so that the miracle can occur. Miracles show that God's power is not limited. God is all-powerful (omnipotent).

Miracles that occur as the result of a happy coincidence could demonstrate that God is all-knowing (omniscient) as well as all-powerful. God knows when it is necessary to act to bring about a good outcome.

Miracles are events that cannot be scientifically explained. If it is believed that the miracles are performed by God, then it is further evidence that God is beyond human understanding.

○○ links

The terms 'benevolent', 'omniscient' and 'omnipotent' are covered in detail on page 38, or you can look them up in the Glossary at the back of this book.

Do miracles tell us anything about God?

People who believe in miracles would say, 'Yes! They do tell us about God's love, power and involvement in the world.' If people do not believe in miracles, they would disagree that it is possible to learn anything about God from miracles.

Activity

Do miracles tell us anything about God? Give reasons for your answer, showing that you have thought about more than one point of view.

Summary

You should now be able to discuss some of the qualities of God believed to be shown in miracles.

5.9 To what extent do miracles cause problems for believers?

■ Miracles and religious belief

Not all religious believers accept that miracles happen. The problems that miracles cause for some believers include:

- God might not perform the miracles
- miracles could give the miracle-worker too much status
- miracles make God's behaviour seem unfair
- the belief that God is transcendent
- the doubt that God would intervene to upset the world he established, having given people free will and the potential to develop scientific knowledge.

Objectives

Examine why miracles cause problems for believers.

AQA **Examiner's tip**

If you are asked about miracles in the examination, remember that not all religious believers think they happen.

God might not perform the miracles

Miracles, such as a sudden unexplained recovery from illness, might happen but there is no proof they are caused by God. Buddhists believe that it is possible for some people to perform actions that could be described as miraculous.

Even if some people are given the ability to work miracles, some believers ask whether it is only God who gives such power. There may be evil forces at work in the world that choose to perform miracles, or give power to others to perform miracles.

Religious believers who accept miracles would argue that for an event to be a miracle there has to be a good outcome. A miracle could never be the result of evil. Jesus himself made this point in one of his parables (the stories he used for teaching).

Beliefs and teachings

And the teachers of the law who came down from Jerusalem said, 'He is possessed by Beelzebub! By the prince of demons he is driving out demons.'

So Jesus called them and spoke to them in parables: 'How can Satan drive out Satan? If a kingdom is divided against itself, that kingdom cannot stand. If a house is divided against itself, that house cannot stand. And if Satan opposes himself and is divided, he cannot stand; his end has come.'

Mark 3:22–26

A *Can miracles ever be the work of the devil?*

Miracles could give the miracle-worker too much importance

Religions all warn of the dangers of performing or believing in miracles. It is thought that the miracle could give the miracle-worker status and fame, and God's message would be lost.

Those who believe in miracles argue that it is easy to differentiate between an individual working for God and someone seeking to gain money and fame. The one chosen by God would not seek fame or wealth.

Discussion activity

The Dalai Lama said, 'Rely on the teachings to evaluate a guru: Do not have blind faith, but also no blind criticism.' Discuss in a group how this teaching might apply to the importance believers give to miracles.

Miracles make God's behaviour seem unfair

Some religious believers worry that miracles imply that God is unfair because he picks and chooses who to help and who to ignore. One person might be cured from cancer by a miracle, while another is left to die. God makes a statue weep, but ignores all the people who died when a tsunami hit countries around the Indian Ocean in 2004. For many believers, this goes against the belief in a loving, just God.

Believers who accept that God does perform miracles think that what is learned from the miracle is as important as the individuals who were helped. The main reason miracles happen is to strengthen faith. Many miracles, such as the Resurrection of Jesus or Muhammad receiving the Qur'an, are for the benefit of everyone.

links

Look back to pages 40–41 if you are not sure that is meant by 'God is transcendent'.

B   *Does the death of thousands in the earthquake in China, 2008, show that God is unfair?*

God is transcendent

If a believer thinks God is transcendent, then they cannot believe God performs miracles. If God is outside time and space, it is not possible for God to act in the world.

Believers who accept miracles would reply that it is possible for God to be outside time and space and still work in the world, especially as God often works through people. They would say that God is both transcendent and immanent.

Activities

1   Explain the problems of miracles for believers.

2   Explain possible solutions to these problems for believers.

Summary

You should now be able to discuss the problem of miracles for believers and some solutions to the problems.

Hume's argument regarding the impossibility of miracles

David Hume's argument against miracles

Hume called miracles 'a transgression of a law of nature' performed by God or God working in the universe. Hume doubted that miracles happen and did not consider them as a happy coincidence. Hume's reasons for doubting miracles are:

- there can never be enough evidence to deny the laws of nature
- the witnesses to miracles are unreliable
- most witnesses to miracles are primitive, uneducated people
- religions depend on miracles to prove they are true – all the religions cannot be right.

Research activity

David Hume

David Hume is an 18th-century philosopher who put forward a famous argument against miracles.

Using the internet and/or a library, find out about David Hume.

Never enough evidence

Hume's argument is that laws of nature have been witnessed for many hundreds of years. There is overwhelming evidence that people do not fly, appear in two places at once, or rise from the dead. Hume argued that if a miracle is going to be accepted, then there has to be sufficient evidence to outweigh the evidence for the law of nature. This cannot happen, so it is always going to be more likely that miracles do not happen.

The witnesses are unreliable

Hume's second reason for doubting miracles links to his first reason. Evidence of the witnesses to miracles cannot be trusted because they are biased – they desperately want miracles to happen to back up their beliefs, so they may exaggerate or even lie about what they have seen. The same is true of those who spread accounts of miracles.

The witnesses are uneducated

Hume said that miracles are usually reported by primitive, uneducated people. This means that they are willing to accept extraordinary events as miracles because they have no other explanation for them; they have no knowledge of science.

Objectives

Examine Hume's argument regarding the impossibility of miracles.

A David Hume (1711–1776)

B Are miracles only reported by primitive people?

Religions depend on miracles

Hume argued that the religions of the world depend on miracles to prove their claims to be the truth – but, as they cannot all be right, then it means none of them is right. Religions therefore cancel each other out.

■ Arguments against Hume's view

Religious believers who accept the existence of miracles reject Hume's arguments. Their reasons include the following:

Never enough evidence

Believers argue that Hume has missed the point as to what is meant by a miracle. It is something that breaks the laws of nature but is a rare occurrence. Miracles are the exception to the rule so there can never be more witnesses to miracles than to the laws of nature. Based on Hume's argument, the existence of flight cannot be accepted because, until 1903, no one had seen anyone fly in an aeroplane. Does this mean that because more people through history have believed flight could not happen, it has actually not happened?

C   *Do aeroplanes really fly?*

The witnesses are unreliable

Founders of religions warn of the dangers of putting too much trust in miracles, and stress that they must be viewed with great care before being accepted. For example, the Roman Catholic Church thoroughly investigates each claim at Lourdes before it is accepted as a miracle. They interview witnesses and make judgements on reliability.

The witnesses are uneducated

Hume claimed that miracles occur most often in countries where there is not a high level of education or scientific knowledge. Events are therefore interpreted differently because of the witnesses' understanding of the world. This is a difficult reason for most people to accept, even if they are not religious, as they know that most nations have recorded the occurrence of miracles, regardless of their level of education.

Religions depend on miracles

Hume suggested that all the religions depend on miracles for evidence of their teachings and the existence of God. This is not true. In the religions that accept miracles, they mostly just support the beliefs and teachings of the faith. Many religions do not depend on miracles as proof of their teachings. Nor are religions in competition with regard to their miracles.

Summary

You should now be able to discuss Hume's arguments for doubting miracles and the response of believers to his arguments.

Activities

1   Explain Hume's reasons for doubting that miracles happen.

2   Explain how religious believers answer Hume's reasons.

AQA   *Examiner's tip*

When you are discussing arguments, make sure that you use words to show another side of the argument or another point of view, such as 'however' or 'on the other hand' or 'some people think'.

AQA **Examiner's tip**

Remember to support your answers with examples of miracles.

Miracles – summary

For the examination you should now be able to:

✔ explain what is meant by a 'miracle'

✔ provide examples of miracles from scripture, tradition, history and experience

✔ explain the evidence of and for miracles

✔ explain what is learned about God from miracles

✔ evaluate whether or not God works in the world and humans can perform miracles

✔ evaluate the problems of miracles for believers

✔ evaluate Hume's argument about the impossibility of miracles.

Sample answer

1 Write an answer to the following examination question:

'Miracles never happen.' Do you agree? Give reasons for your answer, showing that you have thought about more than one point of view. Refer to religious arguments in your answer.

(6 marks)

2 Read the following sample answer:

> I agree that miracles never happen. I don't think statues cry and drink milk. People are making it up because they want to get on telly or make some money. Miracles in holy books come from a long time ago and people thought they were miracles but we know that they are caused by science.
>
> Some people do think miracles happen because they believe in God. God did the miracle so it must be true, like when Jesus healed people or Muhammad got the Qur'an. I do not think they were right.

3 With a partner, discuss the sample answer. Do you think that there are other things that the student could have included in the answer? You will not be able to credit any argument or evidence you think is not correct.

4 What mark would you give this answer out of 6? (Look at the mark scheme in the Introduction on page 7 (AO2) before you attempt this.) What are the reasons for the mark you have given?

AQA Examination-style questions

1 Look at the illustration and answer the following questions.

A *Miracles show that God works in the world*

(a) What is meant by the term 'miracle'?   *(2 marks)*

(b) Describe briefly an event that some people regard as a miracle.   *(3 marks)*

(c) Explain what religious believers think miracles teach about God.   *(4 marks)*

(d) 'God does not perform miracles.' What do you think? Explain your opinion. *(3 marks)*

(e) 'Hume was right to claim that miracles do not happen.' Do you agree?
     Give reasons for your answer, showing that you have thought about more
     than one point of view. Refer to religious arguments in your answer.   *(6 marks)*

Examiner's tip Remember that when you are given a statement and asked 'do you agree?' you must
show what you think and the reasons why other people might take a different view. If
your answer is one-sided, you can only achieve a maximum of 4 marks. If you make no
comment about religious belief or practice, you will achieve no more than 3 marks.

6.1 What is meant by truth?

The nature of truth

We all know what we mean when we say that something is true, but to define what we mean by 'truth' is difficult. When we say something is true, we mean that we think it is right and that there is **evidence** to support our opinion. This evidence may be objective evidence that it is based on fact and is not based on personal opinion, or it may be subjective evidence that is based on personal opinion. People use evidence as proof to establish a fact or the truth of a statement. The type of evidence that is used to prove something is true can be placed in categories, for example scientific, historical and religious.

Scientific truth

Many people will only accept the truth of something when it is proved true using scientific evidence. Scientists use observation, hypothesis (an idea based on known facts that are yet to be proved), experiment and repeated testing to prove something is true. Scientific truths are objective because they are not just one person's opinion. Scientific truth is constantly changing because observation and experiment may result in new evidence that proves earlier scientific **theories** untrue or inaccurate. For many people, scientific truths are the most trustworthy type of truth because of the painstaking evidence used to support them.

Objectives

Investigate what is meant by truth.

Key terms

Evidence: facts that can indicate whether something is true.

Theory: a hypothesis that explains facts that are widely accepted or well-tested.

links

Look back to pages 8–9 for a discussion on proof.

Discussion activity

1 With a partner, discuss whether or not there are things that can never be proved true or false. You must include specific examples in your discussion to support your points.

A Scientists use experiment and observation to prove a hypothesis

Historical truth

Historians use evidence from the time they are researching to discover the truth about an event or historical era. This evidence may consist of objects used or documents written by people living at the time or, more recently, sound recordings and film. Some historical facts can be supported by evidence that all historians can agree on. But a historian also has to explain *why* things happened, and different historians may use the same evidence but reach different conclusions about an event or the era. Because of this, historical truths are regarded as subjective; a historical truth cannot be proved in the same way as a scientific truth.

B *Why did the dinosaurs die out?*

Activities

1 List the evidence that a scientist might use to prove that the dinosaurs died out before human life began.

2 List the evidence that a historian might use to prove that Germany was defeated in the Second World War.

Discussion activity

2 As a whole class, discuss why the truths that dinosaurs are extinct and Germany was defeated are objective, whereas a historian's reasons why Germany was defeated are subjective.

Religious truth

Religious truth is what believers claim to be true about the existence of God, the origin of the universe and the purpose of life. The evidence they use to support a particular religious truth involves experience, belief, trust and faith. When believers make claims about the truth of their religious beliefs, they offer evidence drawn from religious authority revealed through sacred writings, their conscience, religious experience, the history of the religion, and from observation of the natural world. However, the main source of evidence that believers use to support the truth of their religion is their faith.

links

Look back to page 23 to remind yourself of what is meant by conscience.

AQA   *Examiner's tip*

It is useful to understand the differences between scientific, historical and religious evidence, but you will only be examined on scientific and religious truth.

Activities

3 'The moon is made of cream cheese.' How might scientists establish that this statement is not true?

4 'Charles I was beheaded.' How might historians establish the truth of this statement?

5 'God exists.' How might a religious believer establish the truth of this statement?

Summary

You should now be able to discuss what is meant by truth and be aware of different kinds of truth.

Origins of the universe

The Big Bang theory

The Big Bang theory is an explanation for the origin of the universe and the development of the laws of physics and chemistry. It is thought to have taken place some 10 to 15 billion years ago. It is a theory that supports the idea of an ever-changing universe because the universe is still evolving. The universe is continuing to expand out from the point at which it began.

A *The Milky Way is the galaxy in which we live*

After approximately half a million years, the temperatures had cooled sufficiently to allow the gases, hydrogen and helium to form. It took another billion years before the stars and galaxies began to appear. Many of these stars died before our own sun and its planets were formed in the Milky Way galaxy. Some scientists believe that it was the death of the early stars that provided the materials needed for life to develop on earth.

The creation account – Genesis 1 and 2:1–3

The Genesis account of creation explains that in the beginning there was darkness and God. Then, at God's command, the process of creation out of nothing began. It started with the creation of light, followed by the separation of heaven and earth, and then land and sea. Life began in the sea and gradually developed until humans were formed by God. According to the Genesis account, the process of creation took six days. On day seven, God rested and thought the creation was good.

Believers' views of Genesis

The Genesis account of creation is found in the scriptures of both Christians and Jews. Whether they accept both the Genesis account and the Big Bang theory as true depends on how they interpret these scriptures.

Objectives

Compare and contrast the Big Bang theory and the Genesis creation story as explanations for the origins of the universe.

Key terms

Creationism: a view which only accepts that God created the universe, as laid down in the sacred text followed by the believer (e.g. Book of Genesis).

AQA **Examiner's tip**

Make sure that you are able to explain both the Big Bang theory and the Genesis account of creation in the examination.

∞ links

The Big Bang theory was introduced and defined on page 14, or you can look it up in the Glossary at the back of this book.

Fundamentalist view

A fundamentalist approach to scripture teaches that it is the direct Word of God, dictated to the writers as if by a heavenly voice. Therefore, everything in the scripture is the literal, exact truth. It is a factual historical record. Because the Genesis account states that the world was created in six days, then it was created in six days. If the Big Bang theory contradicts Genesis, then the Big Bang theory is wrong. This belief that the creation account in Genesis is the true account, in the sense of a true scientific account, is known as **creationism**.

Non-literal view

Judaism has a long tradition of not interpreting the creation account of Genesis literally, and many Christians share this view. They believe that the writers did not record God's message word for word but brought their own personalities and writing styles to each event. For these believers, the writers were inspired by God but what they wrote in scripture is God's Word interpreted, so that the meaning is clear to the people. The Genesis account teaches a religious idea – that God created the universe – and was written in a way that the people of the time, with limited scientific knowledge, would understand.

Creation account as myth

For some believers, including some who hold a non-literal view, the Genesis account of creation is a myth. A myth is believed to have truth within it, but it is not scientific or historical truth; it is religious or moral truth. It is a story which has been passed down, often through many generations, to help people understand God's role in creation; it is not intended to be taken as a scientific account of creation.

▊ Are Genesis and the Big Bang theory compatible?

Atheists would not find the Genesis and the Big Bang theory compatible as they do not believe in God. They would accept only the scientific account.

A fundamentalist religious believer would state that it is not possible to accept the Big Bang theory as it conflicts with the Genesis account and the Genesis account is the truth.

Many religious believers can accept both as compatible if the Genesis account is not taken literally. If the Genesis account is accepted as a myth, showing religious truth, then it can be compatible with the Big Bang theory. It is possible that God made the Big Bang happen. Scientists suggest that nothing happened before the universe began and this agrees with the Genesis account. The stages of creation in Genesis are not so different from the stages of the development of the universe. There are many scientists who are also religious and accept both the Big Bang theory and Genesis.

Summary

You should now be able to explain the Big Bang theory, and compare and contrast it with the Genesis account of creation. You should understand different ways in which the Genesis account is interpreted.

B   *Stephen Hawking developed the Big Bang theory*

Other religious accounts of creation

Every religion has its own creation story and many have more than one. When an individual accepts one of the stories as true, they are making a subjective decision. Many of the stories fit in with the Big Bang theory.

⊙⊙ links

Make sure that you understand the different ways that things are proved true by reading pages 8–9.

Buddhism and creation

Buddhists do not believe in God and their creation story is based on a teaching of the Buddha. Little attention is given to how creation happened in Buddhism, therefore, accepting the Big Bang theory is not a problem for Buddhists.

The Muslim creation account

The Muslim account of creation is found in the Qur'an and explained by Muhammad. Islam teaches that Allah created everything in the universe and that the creation of the universe is ultimate proof of the existence of one creator, Allah. Muslims, therefore, have no problem in accepting the Big Bang theory as it is additional evidence that Allah is the creator. They do not think that the Qur'an's account conflicts with the scientific account.

Creation story from Sikhism

Sikhs believe that God created the whole universe. God was all that existed before creation. While alone, God planned the universe and then, when God had finished the planning, everything needed for creation was enclosed in an egg. When God decided that the time was right, the shell burst and the elements to create the universe started to move out and away from the point of bursting. Sikhs believe that there is nothing in science that contradicts this teaching in the Guru Granth Sahib.

Discussion activity 👥

As a whole class, discuss the following statement: 'The account of the cosmic egg of Sikhism matches the Big Bang theory.' Do you agree? Give reasons for your answer, showing that you have thought about more than one point of view.

A creation story from Hinduism

One Hindu creation story is that before the world was created, there was no time and no space, just an endless ocean. In the nothingness, a giant cobra floated on the surface, and within its endless coils the god, Vishnu, lay asleep. Everything was peaceful and silent.

Objectives

Investigate the compatibility of other religious creation stories and the Big Bang theory.

A *There are many other religious accounts of creation*

Beliefs and teachings

He makes the night
For rest and tranquillity,
And the sun and moon
For the reckoning of time.

Qur'an 6:96

B *The universe was created out of a Lotus flower*

Suddenly a humming sound, Aum, began to fill the emptiness and silence. The water began to shake and Vishnu woke up. Light began to enter the darkness. A lotus flower began to grow out of Vishnu and in the centre of the blossom sat Brahman. Vishnu told Brahman that it was time to create the world, and the process of creation began.

Brahman divided the lotus flower into three: one part became the heavens; one part the sky and one part the earth. On the earth, he created vegetation, followed by life in the sea, on the land and in the sea. Finally, he made humans.

According to Hinduism, the universe is created and destroyed in cycles, and therefore the Big Bang could be how the universe is recreated after its destruction.

C *Vishnu told Brahman it was time to create the world*

Activities

1. Compare Genesis 1 with the Hindu creation story.
2. Make a list of the similarities and the differences between the two creation accounts.

Extension activities

1. Using the internet and/or a library, find out about another Hindu creation story.
2. Compare the story that you have researched with the Big Bang theory.

AQA Examiner's tip

Make sure that you are familiar with the account of creation in Genesis.

Summary

You should now be able to discuss whether the different religious accounts of creation are compatible with the Big Bang theory.

The Cosmological Revolution

Changing views of the world

In the Middle Ages, religious and scientific views of the world agreed with each other because scientific explanations of how things were included God. However, in the 16th century, new scientific developments led to a change in the way in which people understood God's place in the universe. This changing world-view is known as the Cosmological Revolution.

The Medieval world-view

In the Middle Ages, it was believed that we lived in an earth-centred universe, that is, a universe in which the earth was thought to be at the centre of everything. Science was based on the Bible's account of creation in Genesis. God had placed the earth at the centre of his creation, and he controlled the universe. The Christian Church taught that what mattered was not life on earth but being admitted to heaven after death, so there was little interest in finding out more about the world in which people lived.

The Church taught that God created the universe and, on the sixth day, placed human life at the centre of his creation. Nothing happened unless God commanded it. Everything on the flat earth decayed and was always changing. Everything above the moon in God's realm did not change, never decayed and moved in perfect circles around the earth. Everything happened for a purpose. The Church explained this purpose in religious terms. All knowledge was subject to the Church's control. The authority of the Bible was regarded as final and it was interpreted to support an earth-centred universe.

The Cosmological Revolution

Towards the end of the Middle Ages, the attitude to learning changed. Ideas were no longer accepted simply because that was the way it had always been. The Church's control on ideas was breaking down. There was a new interest in learning, including the study of astronomy and science. This led to new scientific findings that began to cause a division between religious and scientific teaching.

Objectives

Investigate the Cosmological Revolution.

⚭ links

Look back to pages 10–11 to remind yourself of the Cosmological argument.

⚭ links

An outline of the Genesis 1 account of creation can be found on page 120. Make sure that you know what is taught about God's role in creation in Genesis 1.

Extension activity

Using the internet and/or a library, find out how Aristotle's world-view influenced medieval thinking about the world.

Research activity 🔍

1 Using the internet and/or a library, find out why we no longer accept that the earth is flat. Make brief notes on the evidence that has been put forward.

Case study

Galilei Galileo (1564–1642)

Galileo's observations of the universe through a telescope supported the findings of Copernicus. For Galileo, the heavenly bodies in the universe were not made of a substance that was superior to the earth. He observed sunspots, and these proved that the heavens were not unchanging. He proved that the movement of the planets was natural and not the result of God. However, Galileo was not seeking to disprove the existence of God.

A *Galileo used a telescope to observe the universe*

Nicholas Copernicus (1473–1543)

Copernicus was an astronomer. He was employed by the Church to produce an accurate calendar. Through his mathematical observations of the planets, Copernicus concluded that the earth went around the sun along with the other planets. Only the moon revolved around the earth. Copernicus said that the sun was at the centre of (what was then believed to be) the universe and he believed the heavenly bodies travelled in perfect circular orbits around it. The change to this belief in the universe with the sun as its focal point was the beginning of the Cosmological Revolution.

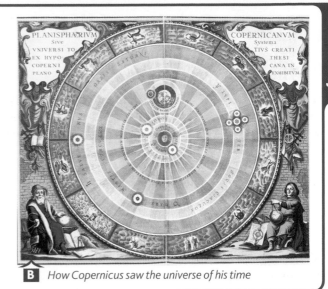

B　*How Copernicus saw the universe of his time*

Research activity

2　**The Cosmological Revolution**

In groups, research the contribution that one of the following scientists made to the Cosmological Revolution. Share your findings with the rest of the class using presentation software.

- Nicholas Copernicus
- Tycho Brahe
- Johannes Kepler
- Galilei Galileo
- Isaac Newton

The challenge of the Cosmological Revolution

The findings of scientists were a challenge to the way people thought in the Middle Ages and to their religious beliefs. For example:

- If the sun was the centre of the universe, then God had not put humans at the centre of everything but on a tiny planet circling the sun. This challenged the idea that God had a special relationship with humanity.

- The Christian faith no longer had control over science. Scientists no longer referred to God to explain the way the physical world worked. Science and religion began to separate as scientists no longer had to make their findings match Christian teaching.

- Religion became the explanation for those things that were still not understood by science.

- God was no longer regarded as immanent and the controller of everything. Parts of God's creation were like a machine that ran itself. God might have created the world and moved on.

Activities

1　Explain why many Christians in the 16th century could not accept the idea that the sun was the focal point of the universe.

2　Explain the Cosmological Revolution.

3　Explain why the Cosmological Revolution resulted in a division between religion and science.

Summary

You should now be able to discuss the problems of the Cosmological Revolution for religious belief.

6.5   Origins of life

The theory of evolution

Evolution is the process by which plant and animal life developed from the earliest and most primitive life forms to reach their present state. It means that one species, or group of living things, is descended from another species that is different from it. A chain can be established going back through time to trace the origin of each species. The apes are descended from another species of mammal and, in turn, the mammal descended from a reptile, before that from a fish, and eventually the chain can be traced back to the origin of all life forms, a simple bacterium.

The two best-known evolutionary theories were proposed by:

- Jean-Baptiste Lamarck
- Charles Darwin.

Jean-Baptiste Lamarck (1744–1829)

Lamarck is important to the development of the theory of evolution. He believed that organisms change to meet their needs according to their changing environment. At the bottom of the evolutionary 'ladder' are simple microscopic organisms, and from these more and more complex life forms developed until at the top of the 'ladder' human life was reached. Lamarck's major conclusions about evolution were:

- the organs that a life form uses the most in order to survive grow bigger and get stronger. Those organs that are no longer needed for survival will shrink until, eventually, they disappear.
- changes that are useful for the life form's survival are inherited by their offspring. For example, the long neck of the giraffe was the gradual result of many generations of stretching and stretching to reach the leaves high up on the tree. Each generation inherited the 'longer' neck of their ancestors.

Extension activity

Using the internet and/or a library, find out more about Jean-Baptiste Lamarck's evolutionary theories.

Charles Darwin (1809–1882)

Darwin's evolutionary theories are in a book called *On the Origin of Species by Means of Natural Selection* (1859). Darwin observed that organisms produce more offspring than can survive. The offspring vary – they are not identical. Depending on the environment, some of these variations will help some of the offspring survive better than the others. The ones that survive will produce offspring of their own. Over time, the number of offspring with these variations will increase and this will help the species to survive. Darwin called this process 'natural selection'.

Objectives

Consider and compare the theory of evolution and the Genesis creation story as explanations for the origins of life.

AQA   Examiner's tip

Make sure that you are able to explain both the theory of evolution and the Genesis account of creation in the examination.

∞ links

The theory of evolution was introduced and defined on page 14, or you can look it up in the Glossary at the back of this book. The Genesis account was also introduced on page 11.

A   *Are humans at the top of the evolutionary 'ladder'?*

Research activity ⚲

Charles Darwin's theory of evolution

Using the internet and/or a library, find out more about Darwin's theory of natural selection. Write a brief account of this theory.

The Genesis account of the origin of life

All life, according to Genesis, was created by the action of God. If the account is taken literally, life was in its final form by the sixth day of creation. Human life was the last to appear. Human characteristics were complete at the time of creation, and humans were made in the image of God.

B   *Is the giraffe's long neck the result of natural selection?*

Beliefs and teachings

God creates humans

Then God said, 'Let us make man in our image, in our likeness, and let them rule over the fish of the sea and the birds of the air, over the livestock, over all the earth, and over all the creatures that move along the ground.' So God created man in his own image, in the image of God he created him; male and female he created them.

Genesis 1:26–27

Are Genesis and the theory of evolution compatible?

Atheists do not find Genesis and the theory of evolution compatible as they do not believe in God.

A creationist would state that it is not possible to accept the theory of evolution as it conflicts with the Genesis account and the Genesis account is the truth. All life forms were in their final form by day six and, therefore, one species cannot evolve into another.

Religious believers can accept both as compatible if the Genesis account is not taken literally. If the Genesis account is accepted as a myth, a story with a religious truth, then it can be compatible with the theory of evolution. It is possible that evolution was God's plan for the development of life. According to both the Genesis account and the theory of evolution, the first life appears in the sea, and the final life form to evolve is humanity. There are many scientists who are also religious and accept both the theory of evolution and Genesis.

 links

The challenge of Darwin's theory of evolution is examined on pages 14–15.

Discussion activity

As a whole class, discuss whether or not human life is still evolving.

Activities

1   Explain what is meant by 'natural selection'.
2   Explain why the theory of evolution is not a problem for atheists.
3   Explain why the theory of evolution is a problem for creationists.

Summary

You should now be able to explain the theory of evolution and compare and contrast it with the Genesis account of creation. You should be able to understand different interpretations of the Genesis account.

The challenge of Darwin's evolutionary theory

Charles Darwin's religious beliefs

Charles Darwin was brought up as a Christian. At first, he continued to accept the teaching of the religion while he was developing the theory of evolution. Darwin believed that the theory of evolution would support the argument for the existence of God based on design. It would show how God had a plan for the creation of the world and everything within it.

Gradually, Darwin became convinced that, although God created life and designed the laws of nature, God had left the details to random chance.

This remained his view until the 1860s, when Darwin's research into evolution and natural selection caused him to reject the evidence for God in nature, and ultimately to doubt the Bible, God and the Christian faith. Darwin wrote his theories about human origins in *The Descent of Man* (1871). He accounted for all human characteristics by natural selection from other life forms, and concluded that humans descended from apes. Most people in his day thought his ideas were wrong because they went against the belief that humans are unique and made in God's image. Most biologists now consider that both humans and apes are descended from a shared ancestor (now extinct).

> " *The old argument of design in nature, as given by Paley, which formerly seemed to me so conclusive, fails, now that the law of natural selection has been discovered. We can no longer argue that, for instance, the beautiful hinge of a bivalve shell must have been made by an intelligent being, like the hinge of a door by man. ... Everything in nature is the result of fixed laws.* "
>
> Charles Darwin

Darwinism and Genesis

Darwin's theory of evolution undermined the Genesis account of creation for a number of reasons:

- Darwin showed how living things developed in small steps, and how this development could be the result of chance. He demonstrated that animals and plants were not in their final form by the sixth day of creation.
- If natural selection occurs by random chance, then this seems to reject the work of a designer God.
- Evolution showed that things changed to fit in with the environment. The environment was not shaped for their needs. This conflicts with the Bible's account that God created the environment for the benefit of living creatures.

A   *Charles Darwin (1809–1882)*

∞ links

Look back to page 13 to remind yourself of William Paley's version of the Design argument.

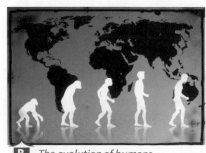

B   *The evolution of humans*

■ Darwin's challenge to religious belief

Darwin's theory is not a challenge to Buddhism as Buddhists do not believe in God. They can accept the theory of evolution.

Religious reasons for rejecting Darwin

Some religious believers reject Darwin's theory and believe that God created humans in their final form. Reasons why they oppose the theory of evolution include the following:

■ The Genesis account states that humans were made in the 'image of God' – therefore, they cannot have evolved from other species.

■ Humans have a spiritual soul that distinguishes them from animals – therefore, humans cannot have evolved from other species.

■ There are gaps in the fossil records that have been found – therefore, there is no conclusive evidence that the evolutionary process took place.

■ Scientists have never found absolutely clear fossil evidence to support the supposed link between the apes and humans.

■ It is claimed that natural selection occurs by random chance, but the advance to a higher life form would require the careful selection of the variations within a species. There is no evidence that this happens within nature.

Religious reasons for accepting Darwin

Other religious believers think that it is possible to accept evolutionary theories without rejecting their faith. They believe that evolution is the process through which God's creation took place. Evolution shows the power of God and God's design for the development of humanity. There is no problem in accepting both the theory of evolution and the existence of God, especially as there are huge and sudden 'jumps' in evolution. These 'jumps' result in unexplained changes happening at certain times. One explanation could be that they are part of God's plan.

C *Is the chimpanzee the result of natural selection?*

Discussion activity

With a partner, discuss whether or not the discovery of 'jumps' in evolution supports or opposes the idea of God as creator.

Activity

'If you accept Darwinism, you have to be an atheist.' Do you agree? Give reasons for your answer, showing that you have thought about more than one point of view.

Summary

You should now be able to discuss whether or not Darwin's theory of evolution is a challenge to religious belief.

AQA   Examiner's tip

Darwin's theory of evolution appears to challenge some religious believers' idea of God as creator. Make sure you are able to explain what these challenges are. Show that you have thought about different points of view.

Can science and religion agree?

A *Can science and religion agree?*

Objectives

Investigate whether or not science and religion can agree.

∞ links

Make sure that you understand why the Big Bang and evolution theories are challenges to religious belief by reading pages 14–15.

Research activities

John Polkinghorne (1930–)

John Polkinghorne is a scientist who believes that science and religion can agree.

1 Use the internet to research Polkinghorne's views.

2 Write an explanation of why Polkinghorne believes that science and religion can agree.

Why science and religion cannot agree

Scientists who are atheists can never agree with religion as they totally reject any aspect of religious belief. Religious believers who insist that their scripture and tradition contain the literal truth are unlikely to agree with science, unless they develop their own scientific theories. For example, fundamentalist Christians have developed their own scientific theories of creation and evolution that support the Genesis account of creation, called scientific creationism. Religious believers who reject agreement between science and religion argue that it is dangerous to change religious truths to fit scientific laws as this leads to the rejection of other teachings in the Bible.

Why science and religion can agree

Many scientists and religious believers have no problem in accepting both scientific theories and the belief that God created and continues to sustain the universe. Many believers feel that the conflict between science and religion is over unimportant points. If the Bible's creation stories are not taken literally, then science can be regarded as revealing the laws by which God created the universe. Islam has always taught that science proves the truth of the Qur'an, and Islam encourages scientific research.

Buddhism, Hinduism and Sikhism all agree that scientific findings do not conflict with the teachings of their religion. In fact, they believe that science has tended to support their oldest teachings and they agree that both science and religion put forward some of the same truths.

AQA *Examiner's tip*

When answering a question about whether or not science and religion can agree, make sure that you show that you have thought about different points of view.

For the two to come together, scientists must be willing to accept that God or an Ultimate Reality is behind the scientific laws, which are continually changing in the light of new discoveries. Religious believers must be willing to adapt their interpretation of the scriptures and their religious teachings to keep up with scientific discoveries.

One recent development has been the theory of Intelligent Design. This explains the features of the universe and of living things in a scientific way, but avoids suggesting that the Big Bang and evolution are random processes. The theory makes it easier for religion and science to agree as it does not say that the designer is God.

Conclusion

Many religious believers argue that it is possible to accept the Big Bang and evolutionary theories without rejecting their faith. They believe that evolution is the process through which God's creation took place. In fact, they say, their faith can be supported by scientific theories as they show how God acts in the world in which we live. There are occasions when science cannot explain problems and so some people turn to religion for explanations.

Religious beliefs cannot be proved in a scientific experiment, but science can give people a sense of wonder at the natural world that supports their faith. Whether someone accepts both science and religion depends on how they interpret the scriptures and teachings of their religion.

B   *Does it all depend on what you believe?*

Extension activity

Using the internet and/or a library, find out more about the theory of Intelligent Design.

⚭ links

Look back to pages 26–27 to remind yourself about faith.

Activities

1   Explain why some religious believers argue that science and religion can never agree.

2   Explain why some religious believers think that there is no conflict between religion and science.

Summary

You should now be able to discuss whether or not science and religion can agree.

Absolute truth versus evolving, changing truth

▣ Science versus religion

The last section considered whether or not science and religion can ever agree. This depends very much on people agreeing that they are asking the same questions about the real nature of the world and/or universe – but in a different way. It depends on what people understand by 'truth'. There are two types of truth that cause conflict between religion and science:

1 Absolute truth.
2 Evolving, changing truth.

Absolute truth

Absolute truth is when it is thought that what is believed to be true cannot be changed. The facts are unalterable because they are correct. For example, it is the absolute truth that there are no square circles or round triangles. Absolute truth is fixed and cannot be changed.

Fundamentalist Christians believe that the Bible contains the absolute truth.

Richard Dawkins argues that God does not exist because there is no evidence to support a belief in God. For Dawkins, this is an absolute truth.

⬤⬤ links

Look back to page 88 to remind yourself about Richard Dawkins' views.

[Beliefs and teachings]

Richard Dawkins supports science

Science offers us an explanation of how complexity (the difficult) arose out of simplicity (the easy). The hypothesis of God offers no worthwhile explanation for anything, for it simply postulates [states] what we are trying to explain. It postulates the difficult to explain, and leaves it at that.

Richard Dawkins – official website

Evolving, changing truth

Evolving, changing truth varies, depending on the knowledge and understanding at the time. As information and circumstances change, what is understood to be true may also change. An agnostic would be willing to accept that more evidence in the future could prove that God exists. For an agnostic, belief in God could be an evolving, changing truth.

Objectives

Investigate the issues of an evolving, changing truth versus an absolute truth.

Key terms

Absolute truth: fixed, unalterable facts. Something which is true for all times and in all cultures.

Authority: something or somebody accepted as having the power or right to expect obedience.

⬤⬤ links

Look back to pages 118–119 to remind yourself about the different types of truth.

 A *What is true about the world?*

⬤⬤ links

Look back to pages 120–121 to remind yourself about Fundamentalist Christian views.

Similarly, most scientists accept that they may not have discovered the absolute truth about the origin of the universe or life. This is why they often refer to discoveries as 'theories' – they are aware that new information may need people to change their understanding of theories such as the Big Bang or evolution.

Some religious believers are willing to accept that their scriptures and teachings are open to interpretation, and that their understanding of the reality of things may have to evolve and change as science discovers more about the world.

The reliability of the source of authority

Whether or not something is accepted as the absolute truth depends very much on the reliability of what is accepted as the **authority**. If a religion teaches that God has spoken directly to people through the scriptures and revealed information about the reality of things, then for the believer that would be the absolute truth. If it is accepted that the scriptures may be interpreted, then what is considered to be the right interpretation may evolve through time. Science evolves as new discoveries are made. For example, in the Middle Ages, scientists believed that the earth was at the centre of the universe. Later, it was accepted that the earth revolved around the sun.

The main source of authority for people is themselves, what they personally believe to be true. This means that truth is subjective. What the followers of one religion believe is different from what the followers of a different religion believe. In the same way, one scientist may interpret the facts that have been discovered one way, whereas another scientist may come to a different conclusion.

Look at picture **B**. Do you see an old woman or a young girl? Your decision will depend on the way you interpret the image. The same is true of religion and science: it depends on what people believe to be true.

B   *Is this a picture of an old woman or a young girl?*

Discussion activity

With a partner, discuss what sort of information might cause an atheist to start believing in God.

Activities

1. Explain what is meant by 'absolute truth'.
2. Explain what is meant by 'evolving, changing truth'.
3. 'Science and religion can never agree as they see the truth of things differently.' Do you agree? Give reasons for your answer, showing that you have thought about more than one point of view.

Summary

You should now be able to discuss the issues related to absolute truth and evolving, changing truth in relation to science and religion.

AQA   *Examiner's tip*

Make sure that you are able to explain the differences between absolute truth and scientific and religious truth.

Do science and religion answer the same questions?

Objectives

Investigate whether or not science and religion answer the same questions.

A *Why am I here?*

links

Look back to pages 130–131 to find more about whether or not religion and science can agree.

AQA Examiner's tip

Make sure that you are able to support your arguments with examples in the examination.

What are the questions?

The last section discussed the difference between absolute truth and evolving, changing truth. It also looked at the ways in which religion and science have similar views on what is true when considering questions about reality. Another issue is whether or not science and religion are trying to find the answers to the same questions.

The answer is probably 'yes', but not in the same way. Both are asking questions about the origins and development of the universe and life, but science puts the emphasis on 'how' and religion puts the emphasis on 'why'. The questions science is trying to answer include:

- How did the universe begin?
- How did life begin?
- How did the universe develop?
- How did life on earth evolve?

The questions religion is trying to answer include:

- Why did the universe begin?
- Why did life begin?
- Why did the universe develop?
- Why did life on earth evolve?

What are the answers?

Science and religion ask the same questions but in different ways. For example, in questions about the origin of life, it is possible to see that science asks 'how' and religion asks 'why'.

links

Look back to pages 118–119 to find more about the different ways in which religion and science seek to prove things true.

Science would ask how life began and seek scientific answers, such as the theory of evolution. Religion would ask why life began and seek religious answers, such as life began because God decided to create it.

However, it is possible for a scientist and a theist to accept each other's answers to the question. The scientist and the theist could both accept that evolution is the means by which God created life.

Discussion activity

Stephen Hawking concluded in his book, *A Brief History of Time*: 'If we do discover a complete theory, … we shall all, philosophers, scientists, and just ordinary people, be able to take part in the discussion of the question of why it is that we and the universe exist. If we find the answer to that, it would be the ultimate triumph of human reason – for then we would know the mind of God.'

What do you and the rest of your class think Hawking meant by this statement?

B   *Is it possible for a scientist and a theist to accept each other's answers to questions?*

C   *'We would know the mind of God'*

Activities

1   Explain the questions that religion and science try to answer.

2   'Religion and science ask the same questions.' What do you think? Explain your opinion.

Summary

You should now be able to discuss whether or not science and religion ask the same questions.

Science versus religion in the modern world

The separation of science and religion

One of the reasons given for science being favoured over religion in the modern world is the fact that the world has become secular, that is, non-religious. Fewer people attend a place of worship on a regular basis, or bring their children up within a religious faith. In the Middle Ages, the reverse was true: religion dominated both society and science, and science had to adapt to religious teaching. The two gradually separated as a result of the Cosmological Revolution, when new scientific discoveries meant that people turned less and less to religion for answers to their questions.

Discussion activity 👥

As a whole class, discuss why the work of scientists, such as Galileo and Newton, has resulted in the separation of science and religion in the modern world.

God of the gaps

As science explained more and more, it was felt that the role of religion was to fill in the gaps that science could not explain. This became known in the 19th century as the philosophy of the 'god of the gaps'.

After Newton's discovery of gravity, scientists began to think that they would be able to discover a set of unbreakable natural laws governing the whole universe. For many scientists, this would mean that the universe was the equivalent of a machine with all parts working together, rather than the creation of God. God was no longer regarded as immanent and the controller of everything. The new scientific world-view encouraged the acceptance of a world that was a machine that ran itself. A scientist called Pierre Laplace (1749–1827) was so convinced that science would shortly have all the answers that he thought there would soon be no need to refer to God at all.

A clockwork universe

Some people regarded the universe rather like a large clock that had been wound up and set going. A clockwork universe does not leave room for the spiritual soul. A belief developed (called Deism) that once God set things going, he moved on and didn't again intervene in his creation. Science deals with the everyday workings of the cosmic clock, and religion deals with God and the soul.

Objectives

Investigate why society seems to favour science over religion in the modern world.

Investigate the impact of this for science and religion.

AQA **Examiner's tip**

Make sure that you are able to explain the influence of the Cosmological Revolution.

⚭ links

Science and religion began to separate after the Cosmological Revolution. Look back to pages 124–125 to remind yourself about the causes of the Cosmological Revolution.

A *Newton's discovery of gravity led to the theory of 'god of the gaps' and to a view of God as a distant being, a creator taking no further part in his creation*

Is there a place for religion in the modern world?

Laplace thought that when all the laws of nature were discovered, there would be no place for religion. However, the certainty Laplace and other scientists had that these laws would be found has been undermined by two recent scientific theories: Einstein's theory of relativity and the theory of quantum mechanics. These two theories have shaken the confidence of scientists in establishing facts about the reality of the world. This means that, once more, some scientists, such as John Polkinghorne, are turning to religion for answers to what cannot be otherwise explained, and therefore see religion as having a place in the modern world.

Extension activity

Using the internet and/or a library, find out more about the theories of relativity and quantum mechanics.

Religion has adapted to the scientific modern world

Many religious believers now accept that science is independent and cannot change its findings to conform to religious teaching. For many religions, this is not a problem. They accept that science has actually helped to support some of their religious truths. Buddhism, Hinduism and Sikhism consider that modern scientific thought does not contradict the truth of their religion. For these believers, science and religion complement each other. Islam has always taught that the seeking of knowledge is required by God: evidence discovered by science is further proof of the truth found in the Qur'an. Most Jews and Christians would also agree with this view.

The modern world needs both science and religion

Many religious believers and scientists argue that the modern world needs both religion and science. Science can explain facts, but the spiritual needs of people have to be catered for as well. Recent research has shown that people who have religious beliefs are healthier and less likely to suffer from stress.

B *Do we live in a clockwork universe?*

Activity

'Science is more important than religion.' Do you agree? Give reasons for your answer, showing that you have thought about more than one point of view.

Summary

You should now be able to discuss why modern society favours science over religion and the impact of this. You should understand how many religious believers respond to scientific theories.

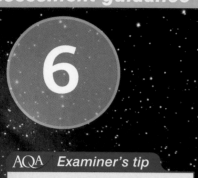

6

AQA **Examiner's tip**

Remember, you may refer to one or more than one religion/denomination in this section of the examination.

Science and religion – summary

For the examination you should now be able to explain:

✓ what is meant by scientific truth and how it is different from religious truth

✓ the Big Bang theory

✓ the Cosmological Revolution

✓ the theory of evolution.

You should be able to discuss:

✓ the Big Bang theory and Genesis 1 creation story

✓ interpretations of religious creation stories and their compatibility with scientific theories

✓ the challenge of the Cosmological Revolution to religious beliefs in the late Middle Ages

✓ the challenge of Darwinism to religious belief

✓ the extent to which religion and science can agree

✓ issues of evolving, changing truth and absolute truth when applied to science and religion

✓ science and religion in the modern world.

Sample answer

1 Write an answer to the following examination question:

'There is no place for religion in the modern world.' Do you agree? Give reasons for your answer, showing that you have thought about more than one point of view. Refer to religious arguments in your answer. *(6 marks)*

2 Read the following sample answer:

> I am not certain whether I agree that there is no place for religion in the modern world. Science does seem to be able to answer many questions about the origin of life through the theory of evolution but there are still things about the modern world that scientists do not understand. Science can tell us how things happen such as the Big Bang but not why, and I

> think that this is where religion can help as it can explain the why through God. An atheist would agree that there is no place for religion in modern society as they do not believe God exists, but there are many other people who go to a place of worship regularly and live their lives by the teachings of their religion. For these people, religion is still very important in the modern world.

3 With a partner, discuss the sample answer. Do you think that there are other things that the student could have included in the answer?

4 What mark would you give this answer out of 6? (Look at the mark scheme in the Introduction on page 7 (AO2) before you attempt this.) What are the reasons for the mark you have given?

AQA Examination-style questions

1 Look at the photograph and answer the following questions.

(a) What is meant by 'natural selection'? *(2 marks)*

(b) (i) Retell a religious creation story. *(4 marks)*

(ii) 'Creation stories and the theory of evolution are not compatible.'
What do you think? Explain your opinion. *(3 marks)*

(c) Explain briefly the differences between 'evolving, changing truth' and
'absolute truth'. *(3 marks)*

(d) 'The theory of evolution is wrong because God created a completed earth
after six days.' Do you agree? Give reasons for your answer, showing that
you have thought about more than one point of view. Refer to religious
arguments in your answer. *(6 marks)*

Examiner's tip Remember that when you are given a statement and asked 'do you agree?' you must
show what you think and the reasons why other people might take a different view. If
your answer is one-sided, you can only achieve a maximum of 4 marks. If you make no
comment about religious belief or practice, you will achieve no more than 3 marks.

Glossary

A

Absolute truth: fixed, unalterable facts. Something which is true for all times and in all cultures.

Afterlife: life after death.

Agnostic: a person who believes we cannot be sure whether God exists or not.

Atheist: a person who believes that there is no God.

Authority: something or somebody accepted as having the power or right to expect obedience.

Awe: a feeling of great respect mixed with wonder.

B

Benevolence: goodness, being all-loving (a quality of God).

Big Bang: the beginnings of the universe according to many scientists took place when a singularity exploded and from this explosion, all the matter that makes up the universe came into being.

C

Channelling: communicating with the dead through a medium.

Compassionate: one of the qualities of God; showing concern for the sufferings of others; literally 'suffering with'.

Compatibility: when two or more different ideas can be used together without problems or tension, e.g. whether a scientific view of the origins of life is compatible with a religious one.

Conscience: the inner feeling you are doing right or wrong.

Conversion: when a person becomes a member of a faith, often following a dramatic change of heart.

Cosmological: referring to the origin and structure of the universe.

Cosmological argument (First Cause argument): a proof for the existence of God based on the idea that there had to be an uncaused cause that made everything else happen, otherwise there would be nothing now.

Cosmological Revolution: development of scientific ideas that challenged religious belief in the late Middle Ages, for example that the earth is round and the sun is the focal point of the universe.

Creation: the act by which God brought the universe into being.

Creationism: a view which only accepts that God created the universe, as laid down in the sacred text followed by the believer (e.g. the Book of Genesis).

Creation stories: myths or symbolic religious stories concerning the origins of the world.

Creator: God is the creator of the earth and of life. (Christianity, Hinduism, Islam, Judaism and Sikhism).

D

Darwin: Charles Darwin (1809–1882) naturalist who developed the theory of evolution.

Design argument (teleological Argument): the argument that God designed (made) the Universe because everything is so intricately made in its detail that it could not have happened by chance.

Dream: images, ideas, emotions that occur during sleep.

Dualism: the idea that humans have two basic natures, the physical and the spiritual.

E

Eternal life: everlasting life after death.

Evidence: facts that can indicate whether something is true.

Evil: the opposite of good.

Evolution: scientific belief that life forms have changed over time, developing from simple to complex creatures.

Evolving, changing truth: the idea that what is considered true changes as new knowledge becomes available or circumstances change.

Experience: knowledge gained by living through events in life.

Experiment: a scientific way of checking and proving hypotheses.

F

Faith: a commitment to something that goes beyond proof and knowledge, especially about God and religion.

First Cause Argument (Cosmological Argument): a proof for the existence of God based on the idea that there had to be an uncaused cause that made everything else happen, otherwise there would be nothing now.

Focal point: the centre of interest or activity.

Free will: having the ability to choose or determine one's own actions.

Fundamentalist: a person who believes in the basics of a religion, particularly believing that what is contained in a sacred text is an accurate, almost factual, record that cannot be questioned.

G

General revelation: God making himself known through ordinary, common human experiences.

Ghost: the spirit of a dead person.

God as the First Cause: the belief that God created the universe. Everything has a cause, so God must be the cause of the universe (Aquinas).

H

Heaven: the state of eternal happiness in the presence of God that Christians believe will be granted to the faithful after this life.

Hell: the state of eternal separation from God, seen as punishment for sin.

History: a record of past events.

Humanist: a thought process and outlook that says that the human condition is what is of greatest importance and that this should be the guiding force behind all decisions.

Hume: David Hume (1711–1776), philosopher and historian who thought that observation and experience should be the foundation of human knowledge (empiricism).

Hypothesis: an idea, based on known facts, that is yet to be proved as being correct.

I

Illusion: an erroneous perception of reality.

Immanence: the idea that God is present in and involved with life on earth and in the universe (a quality of God).

Immortality: endless life or existence; life after death.

Impersonal force (nature of evil): the idea that evil is a power outside of people that draws them to evil.

Impersonal nature (of God): the idea that God has no 'human' characteristics, is unknowable and mysterious, more like an idea or a force.

J

Just: fair or right.

K

Karma: the law of cause and effect.

L

Laws of nature: descriptions of how scientists expect nature to work.

Legacy: something handed down from an ancestor; a way of being remembered after death.

M

Man-made suffering: suffering caused by the actions of humans, e.g. through war, pollution, crime.

Meditation: contemplation on religious matters.

Memory of others: being remembered after one's death by family or friends.

Merciful: a quality of God that stresses God's willingness to forgive the wrongdoer.

Middle Ages: a period of history roughly from the 5th century C.E. to the 16th century C.E.

Mind: the thinking, feeling part of a person; human consciousness.

Miracle: a seemingly impossible occurrence, usually good.

Monotheism: the belief that there is only one God.

Moral argument: the argument that God exists because people have a sense of duty, a sense of right and wrong whose source is God.

Moral evil (man-made evil): the negative results of a bad choice made by human beings by their free will.

Morality: a system of ethics which distinguishes between right and wrong.

N

Natural evil: the harm or damage that is done to people and creation as a result of the forces of nature and the structure of the Earth.

Natural selection: the animals or plants best suited to their environment survive, and those that are not suited or do not adapt die out.

Natural suffering: suffering caused by nature, e.g. because of earthquakes, volcanoes, floods.

Nature: the natural world, the world of living things, the outdoors.

Nature of evil: what evil is like, whether a personal being, a psychological phenomenon or impersonal force.

Nature of God: what God's character is like.

Near-death experience: some people, when they are close to death or in an intense operation situation, claim to have had a sense of themselves leaving their bodies and seeing what exists beyond this life.

O

Omnipotent: almighty, unlimited power (a quality of God).

Omniscient: the quality of knowing everything (as applied to God).

origins of life: how life began.

P

Personal being (nature of evil): the idea that evil is an evil spirit or devil rather than an impersonal force.

Personal nature (of God): the idea that God is an individual or person with whom people are able to have a relationship or feel close to (a quality of God).

Philosophy: literally 'the love of knowledge'. The study of ideas and the nature of knowledge and existence.

Prayer: words of praise, thanks or sorrow, etc. offered to God or to the gods.

Proof: something which shows that something else is a fact.

Psychological phenomenon (nature of evil): an idea about the nature of evil that it is something arising from the mind of a person.

R

Reality: the quality or state or being actual or true.

Reason: A source of moral authority.

Rebirth: being born again after death.

Reincarnation: being born again in another form.

Religious experience: an experience that is outside normal experience, usually involving the supernatural.

Religious experience argument: the argument for God's existence based on personal experience of God through a revelation, miracle, conversion, worship, etc.

Religious truth: truths that are spiritually revealed and part of the doctrine of a religion.

Responsibility: duty; the idea that we are in charge of our own actions.

Resurrection: rising from the dead or returning to life (applied to souls after death).

Revelation: God shows himself to believers. This is the only way anybody can really know anything about God.

S

Scientific truth: based upon observation, hypothesis, experiments and repeated testing.

Scripture: the sacred writings of a religion.

Soul: the spiritual rather than physical part of humans.

Special revelation: God making himself known through direct personal experience or an unusual specific event.

Spirituality: a sense of something which is outside normal human experience.

Spiritual truth: based upon religious authority, sacred writings and conscience.

Suffering: when people have to face and live with unpleasant events or conditions.

Supremacy: supreme power or authority (a quality of God).

Sustainer: God sustains the universe and ensures that it continues – if he does not sustain it, the universe will cease to exist.

T

Teleological argument (Design argument): the argument that God designed (made) the universe because everything is so intricately made in its detail that it could not have happened by chance.

Theist: a person who believes in God.

Theory: a hypothesis that explains facts that are widely accepted or well-tested.

Tradition: something that has been done for a very long time and is therefore thought to be true.

Transcendence: the idea that God is beyond and outside life on earth and the universe (a quality of God).

U

Ultimate questions: questions about the nature and purpose of the Universe.

Unjust: unfair or not right.

V

Vision: seeing something, especially in a dream or trance, that shows something about the nature of God or the afterlife.

W

Worship: love and devotion to God expressed through prayers, ceremonies or religious rituals.

Index